BORN IN THE USA

1964

HOW TIMES HAVE

CHANGED

ONE OF THE BOOKS IN THE

BORN IN THE USA

SERIES

ELIZABETH ABSALOM & MALCOLM WATSON

D'AZUR PUBLISHING

BORN IN 1964
HOW TIMES HAVE CHANGED

Published by D'Azur Publishing 2023
D'Azur Publishing is a Division of D'Azur Limited

First published in 2023 by D'Azur Limited
Contact: info@d-azur.com Visit www.d-azur.com

ISBN 9798866161058

ACKNOWLEDGEMENTS
The publisher wishes to acknowledge the following people and sources:

Time Magazine; The New York Times; The Times (London); The British Newspaper Archive; p4 State Archives of Florida, Florida Memory, https://floridamemory.com/items/show/25387; p5 -donald- - Arrangiert von: -donald- nach der Vorlage von nutella; p5 Pinterestpin/232357662001276946/ (funnyface); p5 Mike Evangelist; p11 Image by Alexa and I by 12019 from Pixabay; p15 (main Photo) Cassara; p19 SSGT. Lono Kollars; The Library of Congress; S Pakhrin from DC (Parade); p25 behrouz sasani on Unsplash; p27 Lucy; Lynne C; p29 Anthony Quintano from Hillsborough, NJ, United States; p34 All That's Interesting; p34 Mike Baird; p34 Alan Whitaker; p36 GLaDOS - Own work Authors own work by Aaron Doucett; p38 Retro Stage; p39 Eric Koch for Anefo - Nationaal Archief; p40 Jordon Kalilich; p40 Jack-in-the-Box; p45 ATM Warehouse; p48 Imbued with Hues/Facebook; p48 Gravity Industries; p48 IfCar; p69 Aldo Bidini; p49 SliceofNYC;p51 Florida Department of Transportation; p53 Lynn Gilbert - Own work; p54 Malcolm Watson; p61 Dustyoldthing.com; p61 Dean Hochman; p67 Quintin Soloviev; p67 Ted Van Pelt; p68 Autoalot.com; p68 endurancewarranty.com; p69 Friends of BNSF; p69 Photo by Tom Fisk; p68 Hotcars; p71 National Weather Service; p74 Nixinova - Own work; p77 Amazon; p83 Omna Tigray; p83 US History Scene; p86 Flickr user ra64; p87 Mtruch; p89 Dallas Area Rapid Transit; p95 Juan Solis; p91 Ethical Trekkin; p91 davidoffnorthide; p95 Corporate Finance Institute; p97 Kingkongphoto; p102 This file is licensed under the Creative Commons Attribution 2.5 Generic license; p115 The Step Blog; p119 Klaviyo; p119 Freshexchange.com; p120 Netflix; p121 Alex Needham ; p121 Willie Duggan; p123 Dan Heap ; p123 Sergeant Rupert Frere; p124 Dave Comeau; p125 John Douglas p127 Alaa Ealyawi - Own work;

Whilst we have made every effort to contact copyright holders, should we have made any omission, please contact us so that we can make the appropriate acknowledgement.

CONTENTS

LIFE IN

Lyndon B. Johnson is the 36th President of the United States.
Johnson took over from the assassinated President Kennedy there was no Vice President until 1965.

In 1964, the United States was the world's strongest military power and life was getting better for almost all Americans as unemployment was down to 5%, wages were up and taxes were reduced. However, whilst things were better for many, the first troops were being sent to Vietnam and as the year progressed so did the military commitment to the fight against the Viet Cong. Students started to protest against the U.S. involvement in this war. A sign of things to come in future years.

4 million babies were born in the United States, representing a birth rate of 16.7 per 1,000 people, which is almost a third higher than now. Average life expectancy was 66.9 years for women and 73.7 for men, compared to 79.1 years now.

Over 11 million people were immigrants, about 5% of the population of 195 million. 137 million of us (71.5%) lived in urban areas as people left farm work which was becoming more and more mechanised on larger and larger farms.

The nation's three largest cities were New York (8M), Chicago (3M), and Los Angeles (2.5M).

FAMOUS PEOPLE WHO WERE BORN IN 1964

Jan 12th Jeff Bezos, founder of Amazon.com
Jan 17th Michelle Obama, First Lady 2009 to 2017
May 13th Stephen Colbert, TV show host.
May 26th Lenny Kravitz, singer and songwriter.
June 22nd Dan Brown, The Da Vinci Code author.
July 9th Courtney Love, singer and actress.
Aug 15th Melinda Gates, American philanthropist,
Oct 20th Kamala Harris, 49th Vice President of the United States.

FAMOUS PEOPLE WHO DIED IN 1964

Jan 15th Jack Teagarden, jazz trombonist.
Jan 29th Alan Ladd, film star.
Feb 18th Joseph-Armand Bombardier, Canadian inventor of the snowmobile.
April 5th Douglas MacArthur, 84, U.S. Army five-star general and hero of World War II.
July 7th Lillian Copeland, track and field athlete.
July 31st Jim Reeves, country singer.
Sept 28th Harpo Marx, comedian and the second oldest of the Marx Brothers team.

1964

In 1964, the top television shows were: 1. Bonanza. 2. Bewitched. 3. Gomer Pyle U.S.M.C. 4. The Andy Griffith Show and 5. The Fugitive. What we ate was changing from traditional home cooked food to ready-to-eat and frozen meals and 'exotic' foods from overseas. Popular were: Beef stroganoff; Chicken pot pie; Frozen dinners; Gelatin molds; Meatloaf; Pineapple upside down cake; Royal Crown cola; Swedish meatballs; Vernon's ginger ale and Waldorf salad.

1964 ROOKIE STARS
SENATORS
MIKE BRUMLEY • CATCHER
LOU PINIELLA • OUTFIELD

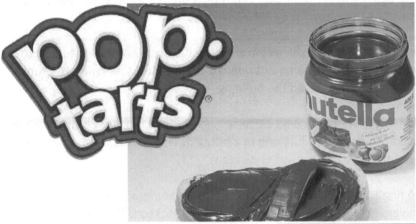

PILLSBURY'S FUNNY-FACE DRINK
Makes 2 quarts
INJUN ORANGE
10¢
PRE-SWEETENED WITHOUT SUGAR
Orange Flavor Drink Mix • Dietary

Baseball remained America's favorite spectator pastime in the 1960's. Americans took their families out to the ball game, and children played on town fields as part of their local Little League or the Senior League.

Television audiences were swelled by the summer Olympics which were televised from Japan. Troll dolls, with their wildly colored hair, was a popular hobby with girls and coin and stamp collecting was popular with both adults and children.

Do you remember these products and brands that were introduced in 1964? Pop-Tarts, Diet Pepsi, Astro Turf, 8-Track Cartridge, Nutella and Funny Face powdered drink mix, and the best selling boys' toys Action figure 'G.I. Joe' and Johnny Seven OMA.

How Much Did It Cost?

The Average Pay:	$6,600 a year
The Average House:	$20,000
16-ounce loaf:	16 cents
Gallon of Milk:	4 cents
1pound Potatoes	5 cents
Dozen Eggs:	54 cents a dozen
Gallon of gas:	30 cents
Turkey:	33 cents a pound
6 pack of beer:	1.75
To post a letter :	5 cents

Education was changing in 1964. In the first half of the year there were protests against racial segregation and in July President Lyndon Johnson signed the Civil Rights Act which abolished racial segregation in public schools.

5

JANUARY 1964

IN THE NEWS

WEEK 1   **"JFK Takes Off"** Idlewild Airport in New York City officially became John F. Kennedy International Airport as the New Year started. Baggage tags that had carried the code "IDL" are now designated "JFK".

"She Loves You" The Beatles made their U.S. debut on a pre recorded edition of The Jack Paar Program, performing their new song, "*She Loves You*".

"Opening The Doors" Harold A. Franklin became the first African-American student to be enrolled at Auburn University in Alabama but needed United States marshals to protect him from a violent crowd as he entered the building.

WEEK 2   **"Nuclear Near Miss"** A U.S. Air Force B-52 carrying two Mark 53 nuclear bombs crashed into Savage Mountain near Barton, Maryland in a blizzard. The bombs were unarmed and later safely recovered but three of the five crew died.

WEEK 3   **"World's First"** The first transplant of a heart into a human being was performed by surgeons at the University of Mississippi Medical Center in Jackson. They took a heart from chimpanzee which beat for an hour before the recipient died.

WEEK 4   **"Cold War Deaths"** Three U.S.A.F. officers were killed after their plane was shot down in East Germany by a Soviet MiG-19 fighter.

"Cigarettes Under Fire" In efforts to reduce smoking, the U.S. Senate proposed increasing the federal cigarette tax from 80 cents to $1.30 a pack and the Defense Department will stop cigarette companies from giving free smokes in military hospitals and clinics.

HERE IN THE USA

"Twin Towers"

The US government has unveiled plans to erect two 1,350-foot-high skyscrapers in New York City to be the home of the World Trade Centre.

The buildings, set to be complete in 1970, will dominate the Manhattan skyline and assume the title of world's tallest building(s), taking over from the Empire State Building. The 110 story building will cost just shy of $350 million and will contain a mixture of offices, exhibition halls, shops, restaurants and a 250-room hotel. The car park will be able to accommodate 1,600 vehicles at once.

AROUND THE WORLD

"Snow less Winter"

In a desperate attempt to get the country ready for hosting the Winter Olympics in three weeks' time, Austrian soldiers have been laying down artificial snow on the mountains, following the largely snow less winter experienced.

Austria has undergone their warmest winter on record with no fresh snowfall for over a month and therefore snow is being transported from the high mountains down to the valleys and smaller peaks where the games will be held. Authorities have assured that there is enough snow, but the process of transferring it is proving to be no mean feat.

THE ROSE DAY PARADE

Pictorial Treasury
PASADENA TOURNAMENT OF ROSES
75th Anniversary

Golden Anniversary

Rose Bowl

ILLINOIS vs. WASHINGTON

50th ANNUAL GAME · JANUARY 1, 1964 · PASADENA, CALIFORNIA · OFFICIAL PROGRAM $1.00 (incl. tax)

The 1911 chariot race.
Chariot races were held between 1902 and 1915
instead of the Rose Bowl football game.

1964 saw the 75th anniversary parade based around the theme of 'Symbols of Freedom' with Nancy Kneeland being the Rose Queen. The afternoon Rose Bowl was the 50th Rose Bowl game featuring the Illinois Fighting Illini and the Washington Huskies, with Illinois achieving a 17–7 victory.

The Rose Parade is an annual parade starting at 8am along Colorado Boulevard in Pasadena, California, on New Year's Day (or on Monday, January 2 if New Year's Day falls on a Sunday). The parade includes flower-covered floats, marching bands, and equestrian units, followed in the afternoon by the Rose Bowl, one of the major bowl games in college football. First held on January 1, 1890 by the Valley Hunt Club, this was always seen as more than a local event. Leading club member Charles F. Holder declared, *"In New York, people are buried in snow but here our flowers are blooming and our oranges are about to bear. Let's hold a festival to tell the world about our paradise."*

The Rose Bowl college football game was added in 1902 to help fund the cost of staging the parade. The first game saw Michigan beating Stanford, 49-0, which was so one sided that it prompted the football contest to be replaced with Roman-style chariot races. Football was permanently reinstated as part of the Tournament's traditions in 1916. Millions of viewers around the world experience the beauty of the floral floats along with spirited marching bands and high-stepping equestrian units along the 5½ mile route down Colorado Boulevard. The parade was only cancelled during the 1942, 1943, and 1945 war years and in 2021 due to the COVID-19 pandemic.

FEBRUARY 1964

IN THE NEWS

WEEK 1   **"Lucky Fred"** Fred Hastings, a 29-year-old skydiver from Louisville, Kentucky, survived a 5,500ft descent despite the failure of his parachute. His reserve chute thankfully opened and slowed his speed to 50 mph, moments before he crashed into rain-soaked ground.

"Freedom Day" Over 460,000 African-American students and 3,500 teachers, refused to show up at New York's public schools, as a protest against racial segregation, closing many schools in Harlem and in Brooklyn. Described as "*the largest civil rights demonstration in the nation's history*" this became known as Freedom Day.

WEEK 2   **"Live Beatles"** The Beatles made their first live U.S. television performance on The Ed Sullivan Show.

"Off The Rails" A 13 month long wage dispute between unions and the Florida East Coast Railway has seen much sabotage but this week a bridge blown up near Miami sent 27 freight cars tumbling down an embankment. The railroad's only wreck-clearing derrick car in southern Florida was blown up. At the Cape Canaveral space complex, 3,500 workers refused to cross picket lines set up by the strikers, closing down 30 projects including the site where the Saturn rocket moon shot will be assembled.

WEEK 3   **"Vietnam Loss"** The North Vietnamese Air Force scored its first aerial victory against a U.S.A.F. plane when one of its pilots shot down a transport plane.

WEEK 4   **"Sting Like A Bee"** Cassius Clay (later known as Muhammad Ali), defeated Sonny Liston in Miami Beach, Florida, to become the heavyweight boxing champion of the world. Before the fight Clay attacked Liston verbally. "*I am the greatest,*" he chattered. "*I am the prettiest. I am so pretty that I can hardly stand to look at myself. I am the fastest. I am the fastest heavyweight that you ever did see. Next to me, Liston will look like a dump truck.*"

HERE IN THE USA
"Car Trouble"

New York City Council have reported over 2,600 cars have been abandoned on the streets of the city since the beginning of the year, a figure considerably up from previous reports.

Although acute, the issue usually occurs in the early months of a calendar year due to the large number of cars registered and insured during this time.

Just 19 owners have used the proper channels, contacting the Department of Sanitation to dispose of their unwanted vehicles, a fact which the Commissioner of Sanitation is 'disappointed' about.

AROUND THE WORLD
"China to Have Last Million Words"

China keeps detailed government records on the perceived wrongs done to them by other nations. The current tally against American intervention and imposition into Chinese waters or airspace sits at 276, and the Chinese claim that there has been thousands of pages of documents being negative of China in both the national and provincial press - criticism which the Chinese do not take lightly.

They add that '*in accordance with the principle of equality among fraternal parties the Chinese side has the right to publish a commensurate number of replies.*'

Valentine's Day

Valentine's Day cards advert of 1883 and a card from 1964

Valentine's Day became popular back in the 1840s, although it was confined to a very specific idea of romantic love. The sending of cards to the one(s) you were attracted to was an acceptable method of making contact, even though it was anonymous. The exchanging of gifts, particularly spoons and gloves, became a way for couples to convey a sense of permanence with their beloved. The mass production of cards made Valentine's Day increasingly popular.

In the 1960s gifts like heart-shaped boxes of chocolate and teddy bears and going out for dinner, or a movie were popular. There were also Valentine's Day special TV programs such as "The Addams Family" Valentine's Day special episode, or Jacqueline Kennedy's televised Valentine's Day tour of the White House.

The Valentine's Day festival itself is somewhat mysterious in origin, with multiple different sources each pushing their own 'truth'. The trail goes back to the Saint Valentine, or one of three possible Saint Valentines, all of whom were martyred. The most recognised saint of the three, defied the Roman Emperor Claudius after he outlawed marriage for young men, by continuing to perform marriage ceremonies for young lovers in the street. He was beheaded for his treason. Others suggest that Saint Valentine was a Bishop also beheaded by Claudius and the third, a Valentine killed for helping Christians escape the cruelty of Roman prisons. According to one legend, an imprisoned Valentine sent the first 'Valentine greeting' to a young girl he had fallen in love with, possibly his captor's daughter, and he signed his letter *from your Valentine*- an expression still used to this day.

MARCH 1964

IN THE NEWS

WEEK 1   **"New Party"** Malcolm X announced in New York City that he was forming a black nationalist party, Muslim Mosque, Inc. "*I remain a Muslim*," he told reporters, "*but, the main emphasis of the new movement will be black nationalism as a political concept and form of social action against the white oppressors.*"

WEEK 2   **"Classy Car"** The first Ford Mustang rolled off the assembly line at the factory in Dearborn, Michigan.

                     "Killer's, Killer, Condemned" A jury in Dallas, Texas, found Jack Ruby guilty of murdering Lee Harvey Oswald, the accused assassin of U.S. president John F. Kennedy, and recommended that his punishment be execution in the electric chair.

WEEK 3   **"A New Attraction"** The first SeaWorld theme park opened In San Diego, California.

                     "Undefeated Champions" The UCLA Bruins won all 26 of their regular games plus the four playoff games of the 1963-1964 season and then won the NCAA basketball championship, beating the Duke University Blue Devils, 98–83, in Kansas City, Missouri.

WEEK 4   **"The King Returns"** Elvis Presley received his discharge from the U.S. Army reserve, after completing of six years of active and reserve duty.

                     "Massive Quake" At 5:36 in the afternoon on Good Friday, the Great Alaskan earthquake, recorded at up to 9.2 on the Richter scale, the most powerful earthquake in the U.S., struck the city of Anchorage, Alaska. 131 people died, and the resulting tsunami struck the coasts of Alaska, British Columbia, Washington, Oregon, and California, as well as forcing the call for 300,000 residents of Hawaii to evacuate. Valdez, Alaska, was so unsafe that the entire town centre was moved to a location 4 miles inland.

HERE IN THE USA

"Battle of the Tins"

The U.S. Government, and in particular the Department of Agriculture, is in the middle of a 'chicken soup war' over how much meat there should be in a tin of chicken soup.

Although the whole chicken soup industry is under scrutiny, the focus is placed on the 'chicken noodle soup'. Under the law, a tin of 'wet' or liquid chicken noodle soup must contain at least 2% by weight of chicken meat but there is a loophole in the law which does not demand the same minimum standard in a tin or packet of dehydrated soup.

AROUND THE WORLD

"No Daffodil on the Coin"

In Canada, patriotic fervour has been aroused by the omission of the daffodil from the design of the newly minted silver dollar commemorating the visit of the Fathers of Confederation to Charlottetown and Quebec City in 1864.

The coin contains the French fleurs-de-lys, the English rose, the Scottish thistle and the Irish Shamrock, but a Welsh reference is conspicuously absent. If no daffodil is added to a second minting the Canadian Prime Minister is unlikely to find 'a welcome in the valley' next time he visits Wales!

St Patrick's Day Parade

The Parade is organized by the Irish Community of New York City to honor Saint Patrick, the Patron Saint of Ireland, while celebrating their Irish culture and heritage. Led each year by a Grand Marshal, and representatives from across the uniformed services in New York City, in particular the NYPD and the Fire Department, each of which have a significant affinity to the Irish community in New York. The parade which is televised on national TV, also features participants from both national and the city's political establishment as well as those from Ireland.

St. Patrick's Day in Ireland started as a religious feast day commemorating the death of St. Patrick in the fifth century. Patrick is said to have brought Christianity to Ireland, and, in due course, became the nation's patron saint. The day's importance was confirmed in 1631 when it was recognized by the Vatican.

The first St. Patrick's Day celebration in the U.S. took place in Boston in 1737 and parading began amongst Irish Catholic members of the British Army in New York in 1766. As the number of Irish immigrants increased in the 1800s, St. Patrick's Day celebrations spread to the streets of major Irish cities such as Boston, Chicago, and New York.

In the 20th century St. Patrick's Day became a marketing bonanza with greetings cards, imported Irish shamrocks, Guinness and a meal of corned beef and cabbage. With many Americans claiming Irish descent and assisted by a network of Irish societies St. Patrick's Day celebrations have spread across the nation.

IN THE NEWS

WEEK 1 **"Beatlemania"** The Beatles held the top five positions in the Billboard Top 40 singles as listed on April 4. They were: "Can't Buy Me Love", "Twist and Shout", "She Loves You", "I Want to Hold Your Hand", and "Please Please Me". A journalist noted that "*No one had ever done anything even close to this before, and it is doubtful the conditions will ever exist for anyone to do it again.*" The Beatles also held the 41st, 46th, 58th, 65th, 68th and 79th spots in the Hot 100.

WEEK 2 **"Oscar For Poitier"** At the 36th Academy Awards ceremony, Sidney Poitier became the first black person to win an Oscar in the category 'Best Actor in a Leading Role'.

"Master Class" Arnold Palmer became the first four-time winner of the Augusta Masters, shooting a 12 under 276, six shots clear of Dave Marr and Jack Nicklaus who tied for second. Palmer won $20,000.

WEEK 3 **"95 Mile Detour Saved"** Crossing the mouth of Chesapeake Bay the 17.6-mile-long Chesapeake Bay Bridge –Tunnel toll road was opened to traffic after four years and $200 million of construction. It replaced the car ferry.

WEEK 4 **"Rising Crime"** The American Bar Association revealed that crime in the U.S. is multiplying four times faster than the population and that the "*underlying cause is excessive tolerance of marginal and unlawful conduct, such as illegal gambling and insurance-claim cheating, which in turn leads to a disrespect for the law.*"

"Air Bags" A test crash of an airliner revealed that the biggest success had been air bags that inflated on impact, cushioning the bodies of the passengers.

HERE IN THE USA

"A Bantam's Duty"

Two Bantam hens have been assigned to the U.S. wildlife research station in Lafayette, Louisiana, to sit on a pair of crane eggs until they hatch. The hens were specially selected due to their impressive sitting capacity, and yet the task may prove a struggle for even them, as the eggs are almost as big as they are.

Once hatched, the cranes can grow as tall as 5 feet, dwarfing the bantam hens. The research station however, is not hopeful that the experiment will be successful, but is nonetheless committed to increasing the crane population in America.

AROUND THE WORLD

"The Perisher Valley"

Work is in the closing stages for the building of the highest church in Australia, in the rapidly expanding Perisher Valley, New South Wales. The team is working tirelessly to complete the construction before the onslaught of the Australian winter, which would prohibit them from working for the next few months.

The Perisher Valley has undergone an impressive level of growth in recent years, going from a remote settlement with only nine small lodges just five years ago, to a bustling ski resort today, with two hotels, 50 private lodges and 13 ski-lifts.

NEW YORK WORLD FAIR

President Johnson officially opened the New York World's Fair, with spirits not dampened by the persisting onslaught of rain nor the civil rights protesters, who largely unsuccessfully, attempted to disrupt proceedings by forming roadblocks and staging protests throughout the city. The '*biggest fair ever staged*' as it's been called by the event organizers, is expected to receive over 500,000 visitors on the first day alone, and 200 pavilions are set up and ready to greet them.

The title of crème de la crème of exhibits, however, is won by General Motors, who paid over $50 million, the value of roughly 7,000 Cadillacs, for their stand. The vice president of the company has justified the excessive spend on the demonstration by saying that the money was spent '*to get people in a good mood, to get them thinking big*', and in turn one can only assume he hopes that because of it, people will buy more Cadillacs.

The New York World's Fair was held between April and October 1964 and was a showcase of 20th Century American business and culture. At a time where public consumerism was a policy being encouraged by the US government, the Western world was invited in to see the products of the 'American Dream' and the triumphant success of the Capitalist system. In that sense, the Fair was an opportunity to explore modern advancements in technology, eat and drink traditional American food, and bathe in the successes of small American businesses. However, for America itself, it was far bigger than that as we invited not only the Western World, but the Soviet Union and its satellite states, thus turning 'expo' into a political statement, triumphantly showing off the US' economic boom, and showcasing Capitalist ideology to all major world powers.

MAY 1964

IN THE NEWS

WEEK 1   **"It's Elementary"** Mathematics professors John G. Kemeny and Thomas E. Kurtz of Dartmouth College, New Hampshire, ran the first program written in BASIC (Beginners' All-purpose Symbolic Instruction Code), an easy to learn computer programming language that they had created.

"Vietnam Protests" In New York City, 1,000 students from Yale participated in the first major demonstration against the Vietnam War, marching as part of the 'May 2nd Movement. Student protests also occurred in San Francisco, Boston, Seattle, and Madison, Wisconsin.

WEEK 2   **"Blue Eyes Saved"** Frank Sinatra was caught in an undertow while swimming in Hawaii during a break from filming "None But The Brave". Co-star Brad Dexter heard his shouts and swam out to the rescue.

WEEK 3   **"Supersonic Woman"** Jacqueline Cochran set a new women's airspeed record of 1,429 mph in an F-104 Starfighter. Back in 1953 she was the first woman to "break the sound barrier" by flying faster than Mach 1.

"Eavesdropping" 40 hidden microphones have been found embedded in the walls of the U.S. Embassy in Moscow. These had apparently been in put in place in 1953 during building work just before the embassy occupied the building.

WEEK 4   **"Playing Until Midnight"** The longest game in Major League Baseball history, ended at 11:24 p.m., seven hours and 23 minutes after it had started, with the San Francisco Giants beating the New York Mets, 8 to 6, in the 23rd innings at Shea Stadium. Some fans had been in the stadium for over ten hours watching the two matches played that day.

HERE IN THE USA

"Shot Down"

When Pacific Airlines Flight 773 crashed near Concord, California, killing all 44 people on board, no one suspected what the real cause was.
The cockpit recorder had picked up pilot Ernest Clark shouting, *"My God, I've been shot!"* before the plane went down. Then a revolver and six spent cartridges were found in the wreckage which were traced to passenger Francisco "Frank" Gonzales, who had taken out a $100,000 life insurance policy before boarding at Reno. He shot both pilots before turning the gun on himself.

AROUND THE WORLD

"Instant Igloo"

The Ontario research foundation has developed what has become known as an 'instant igloo', designed to be a great aid to both civilians and military personnel working in very cold climates. The ingenious design is made from a foamy plastic material which becomes a semi-rigid structure once a match is put to it.

The igloo works via an inbuilt heat source which, when set on fire, causes a rapid expansion of the foam into a 3" thick wall. The plan is to make the shelter an essential for the tool kits of all cold weather operators.

THE KENTUCKY DERBY

The 1964 Kentucky Derby was won by Northern Dancer (top). A 1964 Julep Glass (left).

The 1964 Kentucky Derby, won by Northern Dancer, was the 90th since it was first run in 1875. Held annually on the first Saturday in May, at Churchill Downs in Louisville, Kentucky, it is a race for 3-year-old thoroughbreds over a distance of 1 and 1⁄4 miles. Lasting approximately two minutes, the race has also been called "*The Most Exciting Two Minutes in Sports*" or "*The Fastest Two Minutes in Sports.*" It is preceded by the two-week-long Kentucky Derby Festival.

The idea for the race came in 1872 when Col. Meriwether Lewis Clark Jr., traveled to England, visiting Epsom in Surrey, where The Epsom Derby had been running annually since 1780. Returning home to Kentucky, Clark organized the Louisville Jockey Club to raise money for building quality racing facilities just outside the city on land provided by John and Henry Churchill, now called the Churchill Downs. The Derby is the most-watched and most-attended horse race in the United States, often attended by celebrities including in 2007, Britain's most famous horse owner, the late HM Queen Elizabeth II.

The Derby is not just a race but a festival of fun for not just for those in "Millionaire's Row" - the expensive box seats that attract the rich and the famous and the well-connected - but also for those in the infield, a spectator area inside the track, where entrance is affordable, even though there is little chance of seeing much of the race. One Derby tradition is mint julep, an iced drink consisting of bourbon, mint, and sugar syrup, drunk from souvenir glasses printed with all previous Derby winners. Another tradition, starting in 1921, is that following the Call to the Post, as the horses start to parade before the grandstands, the University of Louisville Cardinal Marching Band plays Stephen Foster's "My Old Kentucky Home".

JUNE 1964

IN THE NEWS

WEEK 1 "We Stand By Vietnam" President Johnson told reporters that the U.S. was "*bound by solemn commitments*" to defend South Vietnam against Communist encroachment.

"Don't Send Troops" In response to the President, Henry Cabot Lodge, the U.S. Ambassador to South Vietnam, sent a cable recommending no more troops be sent to fight the Viet Cong as it would be a "*venture of unlimited possibilities which could put us onto a slope along which we slide into a bottomless pit*".

WEEK 2 "Dam Failure" 28 people were killed, and 115 missing, after two dams burst sending 6 foot of water through several towns, including Choteau, Montana.

"Equality" The 1963 Equal Pay Act took effect this week. Any worker, of whatever gender or color, and who is covered by the minimum wage requirements of the Fair Labor Standards Act, must be paid the same as all workers doing the same job.

WEEK 3 "Barges Damage Bridge" The 26 mile long Pontchartrain Causeway bridge in Louisiana was hit by two colliding barges which created a 240-foot wide hole through which a Continental Trailways bus fell into the water and six passengers drowned.

"Less Car Pollution" New regulations requiring motor vehicles to include a catalytic converter, or another emissions control device, came into force in California.

WEEK 4 "Cancer Warning" This week's ruling from the Federal Trade Commission required that from January 1st next year, all cigarette package labels should include a warning, displayed "clearly and prominently", that cigarette smoking could cause death from cancer and other diseases.

HERE IN THE USA

"Sterilising Starlings"

The latest development in the war against starlings is a new chemical designed to sterilise the birds during their mating season. There are estimated to be over 500 million in the U.S., causing in excess of $50 million worth of damage every year to crops.

The birds are not native to America, and were brought over from Britain by an avid Shakespeare fan, who wanted the U.S. to experience the birds spoken about in the playwrights' work. In Washington, 100 public buildings are wired to give starlings an electric shock when they alight on any ledges.

AROUND THE WORLD

"As Slow as a Tortoise"

In a strange protest, trade union workers flooded the Plaza de Mayo in Buenos Aires, where the government house is located, with tortoises, which explained the recent days sharp increase in purchases of the animal.

The creatures were all inscribed with slogans across their shells showing phrases such as '*We are the government*' and '*the government on the march.*' President Illlia has often been presented by cartoonists as a tortoise because of his slow handling of pressing issues. As police cleared away the animals, people congregated at the side of the Plaza and cheered.

In January 1964 a report produced by The Surgeon General of the United States, 'Smoking and Health', concluded that cigarette smoking could cause lung cancer, chronic bronchitis and possibly emphysema, cardiovascular disease, and various types of cancer. Therefore cigarette smoking was a health hazard of sufficient importance to warrant appropriate remedial action. In June, the Federal Trade Commission stated that cigarette manufacturers from January 1st 1965 must "*clearly and prominently*" place a warning on packages of cigarettes stating *"Caution: Cigarette Smoking May Be Hazardous to Your Health"*, and also from July 1965 in all cigarette advertising.

Prior to this report, people did think that smoking might have some negative effects, but manufacturers' advertisements often featured medical professionals downplaying these thoughts and made the link between smoking and having an attractive lifestyle. They also stated that 'better tobacco' or 'filters' would minimise any perceived problems. The Surgeon General's report also failed to say that nicotine was addictive, possibly as the advisory committee were largely smokers themselves.

There was vocal opposition to the federal legislation requiring a warning on the side of cigarette packs The staunchest opponents were not just the cigarette manufacturers and tobacco state congressmen, but also the American Medical Association, which claimed that the public was already well informed about the dangers of smoking. There was a dramatic increase in advertising claims by the tobacco companies implying that filtered cigarettes were safer than non-filtered ones. The tobacco industry also advertised that it would give $18 million of research funding to the American Medical Association, the only organisation not to endorse the 1964 report, to research, identify and remove, any harmful ingredients from cigarette smoke suggesting that a 'safe' cigarette could be produced.

IN THE NEWS

WEEK 1   **"Service Please"** After watching the signing of the Civil Rights Act on national television, Robert Ingraham and Prince McIntosh, two African-Americans in Jacksonville, Florida, were the first to test the desegregation law. They went to a cafeteria where they had previously been refused service and then arrested. This time, upon entering, they were asked "*May I help you?*" by a white employee behind the counter.

WEEK 2   **"Moving Home"** Gawking sightseers outside their N. Street property have forced Jacqueline Kennedy, Caroline, and John Jr. to sell up and will move to Manhattan

WEEK 3   **"Riots In New York"** After police shot teenager James Powell, 4,000 protesters assembled outside the Harlem precinct police station to demonstrate against police brutality. When the NYPD arrested the leaders, the crowd began throwing bricks and Molotov cocktails at the station. Over the next six days, one person died, 140 were injured, 520 people arrested and over 500 businesses and buildings were looted and vandalized.

WEEK 4   **"Rescue At Sea"** After being forced to abandon their yacht over a week ago, four men from Connecticut, were rescued alive by an American merchant ship, after their raft was spotted by a U.S. Navy plane about 420 miles off the Atlantic coast.

                 "More Troops" Plans have been announced to send 5,000 more troops to South Vietnam, bringing the total U.S. forces in Vietnam to 21,000.

                 "Moon Shots" The U.S. lunar orbiter Ranger 7 sent back "*history's first close-up photographs of the moon*", with 4,316 images, up to 1,000 times clearer than any from telescopes on earth.

HERE IN THE USA

"US Civil Rights"

President Johnson has signed the US Civil Rights Act of 1964, officially bringing the Act into fruition. In a triumphant speech to Congress, the President spoke of the time, some 188 years ago, when *'a small band of valiant men began a struggle for freedom with the writing of the Declaration of Independence'*.

That struggle, he said, was a *'turning point in history'*, and now, in a similar vein, this new act will ensure *'fair and equal treatment for all people in America and continue the ongoing process of racial desegregation across the country. '*

AROUND THE WORLD

"Kenyan Sorcery"

In a drive to remove sorcery from the country, the Kenyan African National Union has ordered over 200 witch doctors to hand over their potions and renounce their practices. The group, including 27 women, gathered at a public meeting in Baricho, where they confessed to practicing witchcraft and laid their tools at their feet, to be collected by Kenyan authorities.

One man confessed to the murder of over nine people *'by means of bewitchment'* and his promise to never *'practice again'*, gained a large cheer from the crowd of over 3,000 spectators who had gathered.

INDEPENDENCE DAY

Independence Day commemorates the Declaration of Independence of July 2nd 1776 , which declared that the thirteen colonies were no longer subject to rule of the monarch of Britain, King George III, and were now united, free, and independent states. A year later on the 4th July, which was that date when final wording of the declaration was agreed, thirteen gunshots were fired in celebration of the first anniversary in Bristol, Rhode Island. In Philadelphia there was an official dinner for the Continental Congress, toasts, 13-gun salutes, speeches, prayers, music, parades, troop reviews, and fireworks. In Paris, France, ambassadors John Adams and Benjamin Franklin held a dinner for their fellow Americans.

Now, our National Day is a paid, federal vacation which families often celebrate with a picnic or barbecue with red, white and blue decorations. In the morning many cities hold parades, with fireworks displays after dark. New York City has one of the largest displays in the country with other massive shows in Seattle on Lake Union, San Diego over Mission Bay, Boston on the Charles River, Philadelphia over the Philadelphia Museum of Art, San Francisco over the San Francisco Bay and on the National Mall in Washington, D.C.

The first week of July is typically one of the busiest United States travel periods of the year, as many people use what is often a three-day holiday weekend for extended vacation trips. Not only do we eat over 150 million hot dogs each July 4th, but Coney Island also hosts a famous, televised, hot dog-eating contest every year, the record being 76 hot dogs and buns in ten minutes.

AUGUST 1964

IN THE NEWS

WEEK 1

"Senior Ride" After a journey of 86 days and 3,244 miles, Lyman Frain Sr., aged 80, became the oldest person to complete a transcontinental bicycle ride, arriving this week at the Golden Gate Bridge in San Francisco after starting in Times Square, New York City.

"War Powers Approved" By a unanimous (416 to 0) vote in the House of Representatives and an 88 to 2 vote in the Senate, President Lyndon B. Johnson's broad use of war powers against the Viet Cong was approved.

WEEK 2

"Fewer Fumes" General Motors, Ford and Chrysler announced that catalytic converters and vehicle emissions control devices will be fitted to all new models produced in time for the 1966 model year.

WEEK 3

"Olympic Ban" After South Africa refused to stop its apartheid policy of barring non-whites from its Olympic team, they have been banned from all future Olympics.

"Satellite TV" The world's first geostationary satellite was launched with a dual purpose of televising the Tokyo Olympic Games back to the U.S. and to provide *"an emergency communication link with hard-to-reach Asian trouble spots"* – such as Vietnam.

WEEK 4

"Supercalifragilisticexpialidocious" The Walt Disney movie Mary Poppins, starring Julie Andrews and Dick Van Dyke, premièred at Grauman's Chinese Theatre in Hollywood.

"Mom Advises Killer Son" After shooting his grandma and grandpop, 15 year old Edmund Kemper phoned his mom and asked what he should do next. She told him to call the police, which he did and waited to be taken into custody.

HERE IN THE USA

"Pampered Pets"

According to a report published in the Wall Street Journal, the people of the United States spent more last year on dog food than baby food. The actual figures amount to just over 50% more at no less than $530 million (£189m) and the figure for feeding American cats is an extortionate $125 million.

It is estimated that there are over 260 million dogs, 20 million cats and between 15-20 million birds kept as pets across the country, a figure that counting dogs alone, totals more than the population of the US itself.

AROUND THE WORLD

"A European View Of The USA"

One rude awakening for transatlantic visitors is America's sheer size.
French travel agents have learned to make a point of telling their clients that the U.S. is 171 times bigger than France, but still they are repeatedly disappointed to learn that a morning is not enough to visit the Grand Canyon from Denver or that a horseback ride across Arizona would be no fun at all.
The insular English are forever making appointments for lunch in Boston to be followed by dinner in Phoenix and then wondering what all the rush is about.

UNPREDICTABLE EARTHQUAKES

The most devastating earthquake to hit the USA was in April 1908 when over 3,000 people died and 80% of San Francisco was destroyed.

In 1964, the USA had 992 earthquakes of magnitudes up to 9.2, with 262 of them being over 3.4 on the Richter Scale which means that they would all have been felt and probably caused damage. There was 1 quake above magnitude 9, 31 quakes between magnitude 6 and 7, 65 quakes between magnitude 5 and 6, 51 quakes between magnitude 4 and 5, 246 quakes between magnitude 3 and 4, The strongest quake was of magnitude 9.2 which hit Valdez, Alaska, in March. In August we had 16 quakes above magnitude 3.4 of which 6 were in Hawaii, 5 in California, 3 in Nevada and 2 (the strongest), in Alaska.

Why do we see most earthquakes in Alaska, California and Nevada and hardly any in Florida, Texas or the North East? These active areas which are at the boundary of the great Pacific and North American 'plates' of the earth's crust also have large mountains and volcanoes. California's San Andreas fault line is right on this boundary. Most earthquakes are caused by the relief of stresses which build up as the earth's plates move against each other. The actual timing and location of a stress relief event (an earthquake) is very hard to predict. Each time there is an earthquake the land moves upwards and sideways, which over millions of years cause great mountain ranges such as the Sierra Nevada, Coast Range and Cascades.

Most progress in predicting quakes has been in using the waves from major earthquakes to understand the interior structure of the earth and also in understanding the processes involved in the build-up of stresses and their eventual, sudden relief. There are far too many earth tremors for 'warning tremors' to be useful. In a few cases, notably the famous San Andreas fault, whose movements have been under continuous observation for many years, it may be possible to say that a stage of danger has been reached, but to set a date, or even a year, for the moment of release is another question. So, although we know that there will be another great quake along the San Andreas fault, we still do not know where or when.

SEPTEMBER 1964

IN THE NEWS

WEEK 1   **"Protected Lands"** This week the Wilderness Act was signed into law in the United States, protecting 9 million acres (14,280 square miles) of federal land in 54 different locations, and providing a legal definition of "wilderness". This has been defined as "*an area where the earth and its community of life are untrammeled by man, where man himself is a visitor who does not remain*".

WEEK 2   **"Canyonlands"** Canyonlands National Park was established in Utah as the 32nd national park.

WEEK 3   **"Papal Audience"** In Rome's Vatican, Pope Paul VI granted a 25 minute audience to the civil rights leader, Dr. Martin Luther King Jr.

"Coney Island Closure" After 68 summers of entertaining New Yorkers, Steeplechase amusement park on Brooklyn's Coney Island closed permanently. A band played Auld Lang Syne and a bell tolled 68 times.

"Britain Beaten" The America's Cup was won by the U.S. for the 20th consecutive time since the competition began in 1851. The New York Yacht Club boat, Constellation, beat the Royal Thames Yacht Club boat, Sovereign, in the best-of-seven series.

WEEK 4   **"Broadway Hit"** Following summer in performances in Detroit and in Washington, D.C., the Imperial Theatre on Broadway put on the musical 'Fiddler on the Roof'. The show went on for 9 years and 242 performances.

"Bush Fire" A faulty car exhaust caused a fire in Coyote Canyon near Santa Barbara, California, burning through 67,000 acres of back country, and destroying 106 homes.

HERE IN THE USA

"Crime Solving Computers"

US Police departments across the country are using computer programs to not only help them solve crimes, but to also anticipate them happening. New York, Chicago and Detroit, have installed the equipment.

Each device costs in the region of $300,000 and is a valuable tool used mostly for statistical processes and identifying people, including those with criminal records. It enables the police to check quickly the antecedents of suspects without having to go laboriously through fingerprint files and the like. The computers require 19 police and 26 civilians to operate.

AROUND THE WORLD

"14-Year-Old Channel Swimmer"

An American schoolgirl from California has become the youngest girl to swim the English Channel. Leonore Modell, aged 14, made the 21 mile swim from Gris Nez, France, to Dover, England, in just 15 and a half hours.

The time and her age breaks the previous record, held by Claudia McPherson, aged 17, of Canada, who swam in a time of 17 hours. Despite strong tides and a jellyfish sting, Modell arrived at the shores of the Dover cliffs in good spirits watched by crowds lining the cliff tops to support and cheer the young girl.

NAZI ART GALLERY

Model of the Führermuseum in Linz (inset).
Altausee Salt Mine (main picture).

Hitler's passion for art culminated in a dream to establish the world's greatest art gallery in Linz, Austria, where he was born, and explains his obsession with collecting famous paintings, statues and tapestries from the countries he invaded. A report now declassified by the United States Government describes the extent of the German's plunder, even referencing an attempt to blow up some of the priceless artefacts at the end. Hitler stored his collection in an Austrian salt mine, from where much of it was sold on the black market to fund an underground Nazi movement after the end of the war. As such, many of the objects originally in the collection, stolen from national archives and museums, remain lost. The report, named 'Interrogation Report Number 4', was compiled through a number of interrogations with high-ranking Nazi officials by the Office of Strategic Services.

The 'Fuhrermuseum' as it was to be called, would have increased the population of Linz from 55,000 to over 5 million, and according to Hitler's eccentric plans, the railway line was going to be moved some four kilometres to accommodate the gallery. The glorification of German history played a large part in the art chosen by the Fuhrer and an organisation called the Sonderauftrag was set up to plunder the artworks. At its peak, over 5,000 paintings, 1,000 prints and a large collection of books, tapestries, statues and artefacts were collated in the Austrian salt mine, and the attempts to bring art, and with that, how people were allowed to perceive art, under the arm of the Swastika looked all but certain. Should the advancing American forces not have uncovered the mine, the art may have been lost forever, and with it, centuries of history and national culture.

OCTOBER 1964

IN THE NEWS

WEEK 1 **"League Winners"** The American League pennant was won for the 29th time in 64 seasons by The New York Yankees, whilst The St. Louis Cardinals clinched the National League pennant.

WEEK 2 **"A Flame Of Hope"** Yoshinori Sakai who had been born near Hiroshima on August 6, 1945, the day an atomic bomb was dropped on that city, was chosen to light the Olympic Flame to open the Tokyo 1964 Summer Olympics.

"Nobel Prize" For leading non-violent resistance to end racial prejudice in the U.S., Dr. Martin Luther King Jr. became the youngest recipient of the Nobel Peace Prize.

WEEK 3 **"Spirit Of America"** The jet powered car, the Spirit of America, driven by Craig Breedlove, at an average speed of 526 miles per hour, set a new world land speed record.

"China Goes Nuclear" The U.S., the Soviet Union, the United Kingdom and France are now joined by China, the fifth nation to acquire nuclear weapons. China successfully exploded an atomic bomb at the Lop Nor test site in a desert in the Xinjiang region.

"Mammoth Construction" A construction crew building a new road in Saskatchewan, Canada, discovered the nearly intact bones of a woolly mammoth.

WEEK4 **"No Touch Down"** Jim Marshall of the Minnesota Vikings scooped up a fumble, twisted around and ran 66 yards with it to the end zone "*for what he thought was a touchdown*". Marshall had actually run towards his own end zone and threw the ball out of bounds in a celebration that resulted in a safety and two points for his opponents.

"The Earth Moved" The shock wave from an underground nuclear test in Mississippi "*lifted the ground 4 inches in a ripple that rolled across the countryside for miles*".

HERE IN THE USA

"Not Big Enough for Two"

For 15 hours, two women fought a 'tug of war' over the purchase of an upscale English bicycle for sale on special offer, at a discount store in New York. Encouragement, food and water came from friends and family as neither woman dared to take her hand off the handlebars.
After being removed at closing time, the women returned the following morning, where the manager made them more comfortable with a pair of deck chairs. In the end, the shopkeeper sold the women two identical bicycles at the cut price of $10.

AROUND THE WORLD

"Hyderabad Reservoir Disaster"

More than 1,000 people are thought to have drowned after a reservoir burst its banks just south-east of the Indian city of Hyderabad after 18 inches of rain had fallen in just three days. The town, with a population of 25,000, has been largely destroyed by the floods and was left sat in over 10 feet of water.
Authorities have said that at least 'several thousand' people were still stuck on rooftops and in tall trees and at least 100 of the sick and injured from the town's hospital are still unaccounted for.

Halloween

Halloween or All Hallows' Eve is a celebration observed in many countries on 31 October, the eve of the Western Christian feast of All Saints' Day. Over 1,000 years ago the Christian church used the day to remember the dead, including saints (hallows), martyrs, and the souls of those who had descended to the fires of hell. The early settlers brought the customs with them to the U.S., but only after mass Irish and Scottish immigration did Halloween became a major U.S. holiday and become celebrated coast to coast by people of all social, racial, and religious backgrounds.

The custom of trick-or-treating began 600 years ago in parts of Europe when groups of poor children would go door-to-door asking for cakes, in exchange for praying for the souls of the cake givers' dead friends and relatives. Here in the U.S. it was the 1930s before children would go in costume from house to house, asking for treats such as candy, with the question, *"Trick or treat?"*.

For many families with young children, Halloween activities are a highlight of the year involving not only trick-or-treating but carving pumpkins into jack-o'-lanterns, lighting bonfires, apple bobbing, visiting haunted attractions, telling scary stories, and watching horror or Halloween-themed films. Older children and adults often go to Halloween costume parties, dressed as vampires, ghosts, skeletons, scary looking witches, and devils. Billions of dollars are spent each year. One quarter of all the candy sold annually in the U.S. is purchased for Halloween and billions of dollars are spent on home decorations and even close to a billion on costumes for our pets.

NOVEMBER 1964

IN THE NEWS

WEEK 1   **"No Change At The Top"** In the presidential election, President Lyndon Johnson defeated his Republican challenger, U.S. Senator Barry Goldwater. Johnson won 44 of the 50 states and took a record 61.1% of the popular vote.

      "Smokers Return" After January's cancer warnings, cigarette sales plummeted, but this week manufacturers reported that sales are now above previous levels, but with a big swing to filter brands.

WEEK 2   **"901 to 911"** Last month's Paris Auto Show saw Porsche launch its '901' sports car. French automaker Peugeot objected to the designation with the claim *"that it held all the rights to all car model numbers with zero as the middle digit"*. With only 82 vehicles made, Porsche changed the name to the '911'.

      "Record Shooting" Bob Pettit of the St. Louis Hawks in his 11th season became the first NBA player to score 20,000 points, finishing the season with 20,022.

WEEK 3   **"Bridging The Gap"** The world's longest suspension bridge, between Staten Island and Brooklyn opened to traffic in New York City. At just under 3 miles (13,700ft) long the Verrazano Narrows Bridge saw 100,000 cars making the crossing on the first day.

      "$82 Down" Jack Nicklaus with earnings of $113,284 narrowly defeated Arnold Palmer ($113,202) to become the top prize money winner of the year on the 1964 PGA Tour.

WEEK 4   **"The Race To Mars"** U.S. space probe Mariner 4 was launched two days before the Soviet Union's probe Zond 2, but did not get as close to Mars as the Russian. However, Zond 2's cameras failed, so Mariner 4 was much more useful to see what Mars had to offer.

HERE IN THE USA

"Simple Monument for JFK"

President Kennedy's grave will be decorated with a *'classically simple'* monument that blends in with the contours of the grassy slope of the Arlington National Cemetery where he was buried nearly a year ago. The eternal flame, lit by Mrs Kennedy last year, will be the centrepiece to the monument which contains no enclosures, no tall vertical elements, and no statuary.

A seven-foot headstone engraved with the Presidential Seal, is being built into the hillside. The designer has stated that he wished to inject a feeling of *'serenity, tranquillity and rest'* to the former President's grave.

AROUND THE WORLD

"Crate Flying"

A man has spent $750, considerably cheaper than a regular air fare, to mail himself from London to Australia as a piece of air freight. Reginald Spiers will be questioned by Australian customs officials tomorrow on suspicion of evading immigration proceedures.

The crate he concealed himself in for 63 hours was 5 feet long, 3 feet deep and 2 feet wide, and was labelled as 'synthetic polymer emulsion' in the hope that no one would know what it was. Spiers did not take any food or water, and claimed that although he did not grow hungry, he was *'mighty thirsty'*.

MACY'S THANKSGIVING PARADE

Linus the Lionhearted was the character balloon for Macy's Thanksgiving Day parade in 1964.

1964 Macy's Thanksgiving Day Parade featured giant balloons of Linus the Lionhearted for the first time along with past favorites, Dino the Dinosaur (whose neck was punctured by a lamppost at Central Park West) and Elsie the Cow (both for the 2nd time), Donald Duck (3rd time) and Happy Dragon (5th time). There were 10 floats, 6 speciality units, 7 push floats and 10 marching bands. Lorne Greene and Betty White were the hosts.

In 1924 to promote what it claimed was the "World's Largest Store" Macy's decided to throw New York a parade on Thanksgiving morning. Despite its timing, the parade was not actually about Thanksgiving at all but an attempt to whet the appetites of consumers for shopping for the next major holiday on the calendar, Christmas.

The parade starts at 9am and lasts for 3 hours winding its way through Manhattan and ending outside Macy's Herald Square store. Televised nationally since 1953, over 44 million people typically watch the parade as part of their own celebrations. Crowds grew over the years so that by 1933 over 1 million lined the Manhattan route. Interrupted by World War II between 1942 and 1945 the parade has grown in scope and has been led by NYPD's Highway Patrol division along with featured guests.

For the first few years the parade featured live zoo animals, but they were soon replaced by large animal shaped inflatable balloons and then those representing characters such as Mickey Mouse. In 1928 and until 1932, five of the giant balloons were filled with helium and released after the end of the parade. They soared to above 2,000 feet and travelled many miles. Whoever found them and returned them to Macy's, received a reward of $100.

IN THE NEWS

WEEK 1 **"Military Cuts"** In an effort to save $150 million a year the Defense Secretary is to disband the Army's Organized Reserve containing 300,000 officers and men. Half will go into the National Guard and be trained to be ready to fight at a moments notice.

WEEK 2 **"Nukes Hit Ground"** At Bunker Hill Air Force Base near Kokomo, Indiana. A U.S.A.F. B-58 was blown off the runway by the exhaust of another B-58. The crash caused four nuclear bombs and a warhead to hit the ground. There was contamination of the local area and one crew member died and two injured.

"Civil Rights Prize" Martin Luther King Jr. was presented with the Nobel Peace Prize in Oslo his work in the American civil rights movement.

WEEK 3 **"Snow Then Floods"** The storm that brought record snowfalls of up to 10ft. in northern California, Oregon and Washington was followed by torrential rain as temperatures rose. The resulting floods have killed 47 people.

"F-111 Flies" The first flight of the world beating supersonic F-111 tactical fighter aircraft, took place this week.

WEEK 4 **"Woman Escapes Death"** At least 59 people have jumped to their deaths from San Francisco's Bay Bridge, but Mrs. Isabelle Kainoa was spotted by U.S. Coast Guard boat and it came to her rescue. Kainoa sustained a fractured pelvis, but survived.

"Football Champions" Cleveland Browns defeated the visiting Baltimore Colts, to win the National Football League whilst The Buffalo Bills defeated the San Diego Chargers, to win the American Football League championship.

HERE IN THE USA

"More Presidential Protection"

Treasury Secretary Douglas Dillon announced last week that Secret Service protection of the President will be beefed up—which was what the Warren Commission recommended two months ago.

Seventy-five new agents will be put to work by June, if Congress approves an extra $650,000 appropriation. This, said Dillon, is just the first step in a $3,000,000 plan that within 20 months would add 205 new agents, plus modern electronic data processing and more scientific detection equipment.

AROUND THE WORLD

"Too Much Lean"

The Italian Government has met to consider calling upon international projects to help save the Leaning Tower of Pisa from collapse. The 800-year-old tower leans almost 16 feet off centre and there is an increased risk that it will fall.

The Soviets have pledged support, and the chairman of a Moscow commission discussed methods used to save buildings similarly threatened in Russia. *'In some cases, sandbags or cement were used in a cavity dug beneath foundations'*, he said, *'and hydraulic jacks were used to straighten the walls.*

NEW YEAR'S EVE

New Year's Eve in Times Square.

Here in the U.S. people celebrate the New Year in many ways. Families and friends may gather to share a meal and "ring in" the New Year, often with a toast and a song and watching the New Year's festivities in New York's Times Square on TV.

The New Year's Eve countdown is another essential ritual. We loudly count down the last ten seconds before midnight and afterwards, many people toast with a glass of champagne and embrace those around them in a show of friendliness. This tradition started as a pagan festival in ancient Rome, which involved a lot of singing, dancing, drinking, socializing, sharing gifts, and kissing! Almost immediately after midnight the Scottish song "Auld Lang Syne" (it means "old long since" or "for the sake of old times") is sung, especially where there are large gatherings such as in Times Square, social gatherings, and large-scale public events such as concerts and fireworks displays.

The tradition of 'dropping the ball' started in 1845 in Washington, D.C., then, in 1907 dropping the ball in Times Square on New Year's Eve began. Since 1907 Times Square has featured the annual "ball drop" where a 12ft round, 11,900 lb, illuminated ball coated with Waterford Crystal panels, is lowered down a 70 ft pole onto the roof of One Times Square.

On New Year's Eve, about 70% of US citizens make resolutions where we promise to do something better in the year to come. The most popular are: Losing weight, exercising and healthier eating, saving more money and spending less, quitting smoking, starting a new hobby, spending more time with friends and family. By the end of January 80% of us have already abandoned our resolutions!

1960

May: Russian surface-to-air missiles shoot down an American Lockheed U-2 spy plane. The pilot, Francis Gary Powers of the CIA, is captured, interrogated, and jailed.

Nov: Democratic Senator John F. Kennedy is elected over Republican Vice President Richard Nixon, to become President of the US.

1961

April: Soviet cosmonaut Yuri Gagarin becomes the first human in space, orbiting the Earth once before parachuting to the ground.

Apr: The CIA backed attack on "The Bay of Pigs" in Cuba was defeated within two days by Cuban forces under the direct command of Fidel Castro.

1962

Feb: John Glenn becomes the first American to orbit the Earth, three times in 4hrs 55mins. Faults quickly developed so Glenn had to manually operate the craft for 2 orbits and reentry.

March: The Taco Bell restaurant chain opens its first outlet in Downey, California.

July: The first Wal-Mart store opens for business in Rogers, Arkansas.

1963

June: Kennedy: 'Ich bin ein Berliner' The US President Kennedy, has made a ground-breaking speech in Berlin offering American solidarity to the citizens of West Germany.

Aug: Martin Luther King Jr. delivers his "I Have a Dream" speech on the steps of the Lincoln Memorial to an audience of at least 250,000.

1964

May: 1,000 students march through Times Square, New York in the first major student demonstration against the Vietnam War. Smaller marches also occur in Boston, San Francisco, Seattle, and Madison, Wisconsin.

Oct: Martin Luther King Jr., the American civil rights leader, becomes the youngest winner of the Nobel Peace Prize.

A US plane flying over a Soviet cargo ship with nuclear missiles on deck during the Cuban Crisis.

1962: In October US spy planes discovered Russian Nuclear missiles had been installed in Cuba. Tensions ran high and many thought nuclear war likely. Last minute talks between President Kennedy and Soviet leader Khrushchev, led to a removal of the missiles and an uneasy peace.

1963: John F. Kennedy, the 35th president of the United States, was assassinated on November 22 in Dallas, Texas, while riding in a presidential motorcade. He was with his wife Jacqueline, Texas Governor John Connally, and Connally's wife Nellie when he was fatally shot from a nearby building by Lee Harvey Oswald. Governor Connally was seriously wounded in the attack. The motorcade rushed to the local hospital, where Kennedy was pronounced dead about 30 minutes after the shooting. Mr Connally recovered.

1969 APOLLO 11. Neil Armstrong becomes the first man to walk on the moon. "One small step for man, one giant leap for mankind."

1965: In January, Sir Winston Churchill died aged 90. Sir Winston served as Prime Minister of the United Kingdom from 1940-45 and again from 1951-1955. He is best known for his wartime leadership as PM.

1965

Jan: Lyndon B. Johnson begins his Presidency.

March 3,500 US Marines, the first American ground combat troops arrive in Da Nang, South Vietnam.

March: Alabama sees a series of civil rights marches, almost all of which are met with violence.

Sept: Fidel Castro announces that anyone who wants to, can emigrate from Cuba to the US.

1966

Jan: President Johnson states that the US should stay in South Vietnam until Communist aggression there is ended. There are now 190,000 US troops in Vietnam.

April: There are now 250,000 US troops in Vietnam.

Aug: The Beatles play their very last US concert at Candlestick Park in San Francisco, California.

1967

April: In San Francisco, 10,000 march against the Vietnam War with more demonstrations in New York where Martin Luther King Jr. speaks out against the war.

May: Elvis Presley and Priscilla Beaulieu are married in Las Vegas.

June-July-Aug: Racial tensions run high with riots in Buffalo, Newark, Plainfield (NJ), Minneapolis, Detroit, Rochester, Milwaukee and Washington D.C.

1968:

March: American troops kill scores of civilians in the village of My Lai. The story will first become public in November 1969 and undermines public support for the U.S. efforts in Vietnam.

April: Martin Luther King Jr. is shot dead in Memphis, Tennessee. In response, riots erupt in major American cities, lasting for several days afterwards.

1969

Jan: Richard Nixon is sworn in as the 37th President of the United States.

Feb: The U.S. population reaches 200 million.

June: The Stonewall riots in New York City mark the start of the modern gay rights movement in the US.

In the '60s, home decoration moved away from the dark and sombre style of the 50s and adopted a bright, light and more airy look. New homes often featured large living spaces that could be divided by either 'half' walls featuring a fireplace, or by room dividing units which could be filled with books, a television, a music centre of ornaments. Technological advances enabled plastics to be moulded and coloured and easy to clean fabrics were introduced for furniture.

By the Sixties homes already had many domestic appliances most of which came with a wider range of functions. The transistor allowed televisions, radios and music systems to be lighter and easily able to be moved from room to room.

Mass production meant that prices steadily dropped, or improved models sold for the same price as their predecessors. There would be the main TV but also a portable or two for use in the bedroom or den. Portable radios, cassette recorders, hair dryers, curlers,

and alarm clocks were common place. You probably had a side-by-side refrigerator, a popcorn machine, a food processor, a waffle maker, built in ovens or a separate oven and stove top. Automatic washers, easy care clothing and steam irons made laundry chores easier. Slowly, the traditional role of the woman was changing. Technology gave them more free time. Time for leisure and also to start their own careers.

IN THE 1960s

The Sixties saw a massive change in the foods we ate. Not only were we exposed to foods from other cultures via television, we also were able to buy a large range of ready to eat meals and frozen ingredients, which cut preparation time immensely. Finally we ate out more. The expansion of the fast food outlets meant much more choice than the traditional 'diner' and food that kids loved.

By the end of the '60s there were 250 Burger Kings, 2,000 McDonald's, 1,900 Kentucky Fried Chicken outlets together with Taco Bell, Wendy's, Jack in the Box, Pizza Hut, Domino's, Arby's, Subway and many more.

Located in your local mall or by the highway, you could drive up and feed the family for just a few dollars. Not only was there no battle with the kids over eating up vegetables there was no cooking or clearing up and this was seen as a fun family night out without having to go downtown.

Home Cooking

A rise in supermarkets and pre-packaged food, an advertising boom, an interest in overseas dishes and a wish to cut preparation time while delivering new and exciting food for the family changed what we ate in the Sixties.

Many dishes were bought frozen and ready-to-eat, others were from a mix of fresh and bought ingredients to give 'quick short cuts' to producing tasty food.

Exotic and sophisticated sounding dishes from Europe could impress your friends and yet demand very little skill. If you had moved out to the suburbs and wanted to give your new neighbors something different from mom's meat loaf then the magazines were full of advertisements for Chicken Kiev, Baked Alaska, Fondue, Chicken a la King, Beef Bourguignon, Shrimp Cocktail and more.

Some things such as home delivery of milk and the ice cream truck have disappeared. Small neighborhood stores lost out to the supermarket and shopping mall outlets. Things are cheaper now, but are they better?

Tunnelicious!
Pillsbury's New Bundt Cake Mixes:
Tunnel of Fudge! And Tunnel of Lemon!

SURPRISE!
Rich creme filling inside!

Chicken Marengo

To make this Chicken Marengo, you need 12 ingredients.

8 of them are in these cans.

ART AND CULTURE

1960 - 1963

1960
Feb: Norman Rockwell produces his **Triple Self-Portrait** to be used with the first excerpt from his autobiography in the Saturday Evening Post.
Jul: Harper Lee's **To Kill a Mockingbird** is published.

1961 Mar: 'Ken' is introduced as a boyfriend for 'Barbie'.
Irving Stone's biographical novel of Michelangelo, **The Agony and the Ecstasy,** is published.
April: Italian tenor Luciano Pavarotti makes his debut as Rodolfo in **La Bohème** at Reggio Emilia, Northern Italy.

1962 Dec: John Steinbeck, is awarded the Nobel Prize in Literature.
Aleksandr Solzhenitsyn's novella, **One Day in the Life of Ivan Denisovich** is published in Russia.

1963 Jan: Leonardo da Vinci's **Mona Lisa** is exhibited in the US for the first time. It is at the National Gallery of Art in Washington for four weeks and viewed by over half a million people.
Nov: Authors CS Lewis (**Narnia**) and Aldous Huxley (**Brave New World**) both die on 23rd, but the news is overshadowed by the assassination of JFK.

1964 - 1969

1964 Feb: The Indiana Governor declares that the song **Louie Louie** by the Kingsmen is pornographic and made 'his ears tingle'.
Sept: Ernest Hemingway's memoirs of his years in Paris, **'A Moveable Feast'** is published posthumously by his wife.

1965 Fiddler on the Roof won nine categories of the Tony Awards. It ran for an unprecedented 3,242 shows in its original run.
May: The **Symphony of the New World**, the first racially integrated orchestra in the United States, plays its first concert, in Carnegie Hall, New York City.

1966 Feb: Jacqueline Susann has her first novel, **Valley of the Dolls**, published.
Sept: The Metropolitan Opera House, Lincoln Center, opens in New York City with the première of **Anthony and Cleopatra** by Samuel Barber – which is rejected by the critics.

1967 Jan: **Batgirl** is introduced in the **Detective Comics** series. When not exercising her superhero powers, she is head of Gotham City public library.
Nov: The first issue of **Rolling Stone** magazine is published in San Francisco.

1968 Jun: Valerie Solanas, a radical feminist, shoots **Andy Warhol** at his NYC studio. He survives after five hours of surgery.
N. Scott Momaday's novel **House Made of Dawn** wins the Pulitzer Prize for fiction and leads the breakthrough of Native American literature into the mainstream.

1969 Jan: **The Beatles** perform together for the last time on the rooftop of Apple Records in London. The impromptu concert was broken up by the police.
Feb: After 147 years, the last issue of **The Saturday Evening Post**, in its original form, appears.

Doing The Locomotion.

'TWISTIN' TIME IS HERE'

The 'pop market' boomed in the 60's and this brought with it a raft of dance crazes. New dance fads appeared almost every week and many were commercialized versions of dancing seen in the clubs and discothèques of the major cities.

The Twist: Chubby Checker got the hips swivelling in the worldwide dance craze.

The Madison: A line dance that inspired dance teams and competitions.

The Hully Gully: 'Shake your shoulders - like shaking a handful of nuts - and wiggle your knees.'

The Pony: Imagine you're riding a pony! A prancing triple step, mostly on the spot.

The Hitch Hike: Marvin Gaye started it with his song. Thumbs out, wave them and shimmy too.

The Swim: Swimming on the dance floor, maybe the most entertaining one of all.

The Locomotion: Little Eva had your arms pumping round, in a chain formation like a train.

Artist Andy Warhol premieres his "Campbell's Soup Cans" exhibit in Los Angeles.

Andy Warhol famously borrowed familiar icons from everyday life and the media, among them celebrity and tabloid news photos, comic strips, and, in this work, the popular canned soup made by the Campbell's Soup Company. When he first exhibited "Campbell's Soup Cans", the images were displayed together on shelves, like products in a grocery aisle. At the time, Campbell's sold 32 soup varieties and each one of Warhol's 32 canvases corresponds to a different flavor, each having a different label. The first flavor, introduced in 1897, was tomato.

Each canvas was hand painted and the fleur de lys pattern round each can's bottom edge was hand stamped. Warhol said, "I used to drink Campbell's Soup. I used to have the same lunch every day, for 20 years, I guess!"

FILMS

1960 - 1963

1960   **Ben Hur**, the religious epic, was a remake of a 1925 silent film with a similar title and had the largest budget ($15.175m) and the largest sets built of any film produced at the time.

1961   Billy Wilder's risqué tragi-comedy **The Apartment** won the Academy Award for Best Picture. Starring Jack Lemmon and Shirley MacLaine, it tells a story of an ambitious, lonely insurance clerk who lends out his New York apartment to executives for their love affairs.

1962   New Films released this year included, **Lolita** starring James Mason and Sue Lyon. **Dr No**, the first James Bond film, starring Sean Connery and Ursula Andress and **What Ever Happened to Baby Jane?** a horror film with Bette Davis

1963   **Lawrence of Arabia,** based on author TS Eliot's book 'Seven Pillars of Wisdom' and starring Peter O'Toole and Alec Guinness won the Oscar for Best Picture.
The publicity of the affair between the stars, Elizabeth Taylor and Richard Burton, helped make **Cleopatra** a huge box office success but the enormous production costs, caused the film to be a financial disaster.

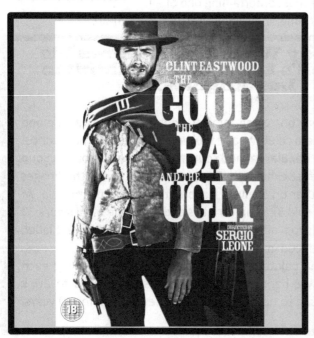

1964 - 1969

1964   The historical adventure, sex comedy romp **Tom Jones** won four Oscars, Best Picture, Best Director, Best Adapted Screenplay and Best Musical Score. Albert Finney starred as the titular hero and Susannah York as the girl he loves.

1965   Winning the Oscar this year, the film **My Fair Lady,** based on George Bernard Shaw's play 'Pygmalion', tells the story of Eliza Doolittle and her quest to 'speak proper' in order to be presentable in Edwardian London's high society. Rex Harrison and Audrey Hepburn starred and it became the 2nd highest grossing film of the year just behind **The Sound of Music** which won the Academy Award the following year.

1966   **The Good, the Bad and the Ugly** was directed by Sergio Leonie, the Italian director who gave rise to the term 'spaghetti western'- a genre of westerns produced and directed by Italians. Clint Eastwood was the Good, Lee Van Cleef, the Bad and Eli Wallach, the Ugly. The film was a huge success and catapulted Clint Eastwood to fame.

1967   The fun filled seduction of Benjamin Braddock by Mrs Robinson in **The Graduate** made the film the biggest grossing production of the year world-wide.

1968   The famous quote "They call me Mister Tibbs" comes from **In the Heat of the Night** where Sidney Poitier plays Virgil Tibbs, a black police detective from Philadelphia, caught up in a murder investigation in racially hostile Mississippi. Rod Steiger is the white chief of police.

1969   **Oliver** the musical based on Dicken's novel and Lionel Bart's stage show, carried off the Oscar for Best Picture.

Editor's Note: The Academy Awards are held in February and each year's awards are presented for films that were first shown during the full preceding calendar year from January 1 to December 31 Los Angelis, California. Source: Wikipedia

THE FIRST JAMES BOND FILM!

HARRY SALTZMAN and ALBERT R. BROCCOLI PRESENT IAN FLEMING'S

DR. NO

TECHNICOLOR

SEAN CONNERY AS 007 · URSULA ANDRESS · JOSEPH WISEMAN · JACK LOI

1962 saw the first-ever launch of a James Bond film in a cinema and was attended by the stars, Sean Connery and Ursula Andress together with the James Bond creator Ian Fleming. The plot of this British spy film revolves around James Bond who needs to solve the mystery of the strange disappearance of a British agent to Jamaica and finds an underground base belonging to Dr No who is plotting to disrupt the American space launch with a radio beam weapon. The film was condemned by The Vatican as "a dangerous mixture of violence, vulgarity, sadism, and sex".

1962 : "West Side Story" Wins The Academy Awards "Best Picture" category.

The musical with lyrics by Stephen Sondheim and music by Leonard Bernstein was inspired by the story of William Shakespeare's "Romeo and Juliet". Set in the mid 1950s in Upper West Side of New York City, which was then, a cosmopolitan working-class area, it follows the rivalry between the Jets and the Sharks, two teenage street gangs from different ethnic backgrounds.

The Sharks are from Puerto Rico and are taunted by the white Jets gang. The hero, Tony, a former member of the Jets falls in love with Maria, the sister of the leader of the Sharks. The sophisticated music and the extended dance scenes, focusing on the social problems marked a turning point in musical theatre. The film starred Natalie Wood and Richard Beymer.

FASHION

It was a decade of three parts for fashion. The first years were reminiscent of the fifties, conservative and restrained, classic in style and design. Jackie Kennedy, the President's glamorous wife, was very influential with her tailored suit dresses and pill box hats, white pearls and kitten heels.

The hairdresser was of extreme importance. Beehive coiffures worn by the likes of Barbra Streisand and Brigitte Bardot were imitated by women of all ages and Audrey Hepburn popularised the high bosom, sleeveless dress. While low, square toed shoes were high fashion, 'on the street', stilettos rivalled them.

THE SWINGING SIXTIES

By the mid 60's, music permeated the fashion scene and how you dressed was becoming all about self-expression and creativity with an air of rebellion. Women's hemlines were shortening until they fell at the upper thigh, the look became sleeker and more modern. At the same time, androgynous clothing was becoming trendy; cut-out dresses that let the skin peek through, just enough to capture the imagination, were prominent and the term 'smart casual' appeared, epitomised by leopard skin outfits made popular by icons such as Brigitte Bardot and Elizabeth Taylor.

Knee length coats over miniskirts, worn with fur hats, flat shoes and gloves were so popular that the look inspired Bob Dylan's tribute song, **Leopard-Skin Pill-Box Hat.**

Men's fashion broke past previous traditions and the younger, free-spirited generation was influenced by the modern music. The Beatles heralded colorful, tailored, 'mod suits', collarless shirts and of course the Beatle boot- the Cuban-heeled, tight-fitting, ankle-high boots with a sharp pointed toe.

In The 1960s

The Hippies

Hippie 'anti- fashion' was booming by the late '60 in the US as a visual protest against war and civil injustice.

The 'flower power' children's clothes reflected their desire for change. Jeans were ubiquitous both for men and women, skin-tight drainpipes through to the flared bell-bottoms of the later years. Bright, swirling colours.

Psychedelic, tie-dye shirts, long hair and beards were commonplace. Individualism was the word and micro miniskirts were worn alongside brightly coloured and patterned tunics or long, flowing, floral dresses and skirts.

Art Inspires Fashion

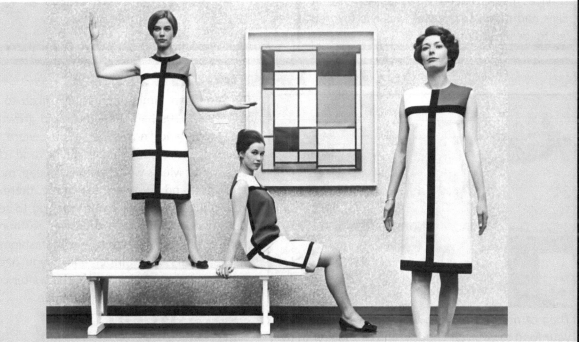

The 60's trend for 'color-blocking' was led by famous Paris fashion designers. Yves Saint Laurent was the first when he designed collarless, sleeveless, cocktail dresses inspired by the work of the artist Piet Mondrian. The bright, colorful, solid squares bordered by black lines evoked Mondrian's abstract canvases. He complimented his dresses with black pumps decorated with a large square buckle in gold or silver metal and often added small ball-shaped hats echoing the colors. The simple cut, boxy shapes, geometric lines and bold colors were so successful, they were quickly imitated 'on the street'.

LEISURE

THE VACATION

Family vacations were mostly taken in the summer while the kids were off school and road trips were a favorite. It might be a journey to stay with family or friends in another State but by the mid 60's, going to Florida was becoming more and more attractive. Here was the beach, boating and fishing.

In 1962 Seattle's Space Needle was inaugurated and during the World Fair, more than 2.3 million people visited. In 1963, the Kennedy Space Center attracted almost 100,000 visitors in its first year and to delight the hundreds of thousands who visited Disneyland at Anaheim, California, 'Casa de Fritos' created 'Doritos' to recycle old tortillas that would have been thrown away.

For the better off families, improved airline services meant that the Hawaiian Islands that Elvis had made so popular, was the favored 'go to' destination.

"EATING IS A LEISURE ACTIVITY"

The American family increasingly liked to 'eat out'. The 1950s had seen the rapid growth of fast food, and now the 1960s were the beginning of casual family dining and chain restaurants. Meals were relatively cheap, menus were short and if you wanted music, there was often a jukebox in the corner for you to select your own. In more expensive restaurants patrons enjoyed cocktails – old fashions or whiskey sours with dinner and if you had an urgent telephone call to make, the waiter could plug a phone into a jack by your table.

Then came the Drive-ins. 'Car Hop' waiters bringing your food to your car window and in 1966, with over 1,000 locations throughout the US, Kentucky Fried Chicken popularized the idea of a 'take away' fast food meal. No long road trip could be without a stop at Howard Johnson's, the largest restaurant chain in the '60s, known for its fried clam strips and 28 flavors of homemade ice cream.

IN THE 1960s

WOODSTOCK

MUSIC AND ARTS FAIR

JIMI HENDRIX   JANIS JOPLIN

♫ AUGUST 15-16-17 - 1969 ♫

THREE DAY PEACE AND MUSIC FESTIVAL

★ **FRIDAY THE 15th** - Joan Baez, Arlo Guthrie, Richie Havens, Sly & The Family Stone, Tim Hardin, Nick Benes, Sha Na Na

★ **SATURDAY THE 16th** - Canned Heat, Creedence Clearwater, Melanie, Grateful Dead, Janis Joplin Jefferson Airplane, Incredible String Band, Santana The Who, Paul Buttrfield, Keef Hartley

★ **SUNDAY THE 17th** - The Band, Crosby Stills Nash and Young, Ten Years After, Blood Sweat & Tears Joe Cocker, Jimi Hendrix, Mountain, Keef Hartley

AQUARIAN EXPOSITION

WHITE LAKE, NEW YORK

Teenage Leisure

The 60's was the era of the teenager, but it started off with the same disciplines as the fifties. At school the teachers commanded respect and gave out punishment when it was not given. Parents could determine when and where their children could be out of house, gave sons and daughters chores to do and families ate together and watched television together. Teens were into dances, the twist, the slop, the fly - not politics and environment and there was very little drug use. However, as the decade wore on, the lure of newfound freedom for the young was hard for many to overcome.

You could get your license at 16, borrow the family car and local drive-ins became the place to meet, drink coffee or sodas, listen to the latest hits on the juke box and talk with friends. The political climate influenced the young, there were race riots and protests, teenagers demonstrated in the streets against the Vietnam War, for civil rights and to 'Ban the Bomb'. Many chose to take the 'hippie' point of view, advocating non-violence and love, and by the end of the decade, "Make Love not War" was the 'flower children's' mantra.

Outdoor music festivals sprang up, most notably Woodstock, and thousands gathered to listen to their favorite artists, rock concerts played to packed houses and the young experimented with marijuana and LSD. Psychedelic art was incorporated into films, epitomised by the Beatles' 'Yellow Submarine'.

1960 Connie Francis had the most top ten hits this year. **Mama, Everybody's Somebody's Fool, My Heart Has a Mind of Its Own, Many Tears Ago** and **Among My Souvenirs**.

Elvis is promoted to Sergeant in the Army and still manages to have three #1's. **Stuck on You** in April, **It's Now or Never** in August and **Are You Lonesome Tonight** in November.

1961 This was Elvis's year. He had six top 10 hits in the US and his **Wooden** Heart, from his 1960 movie, GI Blues, was the best-selling single of the year in the UK and reached #1 in five other countries.

Motown Records sign up The Supremes and **Shop Around** by The Miracles becomes Motown's first million selling single.

At the Grammy Awards, Bob Newhart's **The Button-Down Mind** wins Album of the Year.

1962 Chubby Checker had four top 10 hits in the year, starting with **The Twist**, released in 1961 but peaking in January. **Slow Twistin'** in March, **Limbo Rock** and **Popeye** in November.

In May, Acker Bilk's **Stranger on the Shore** becomes the first British recording ever to reach the #1 spot on the US Billboard Hot 100.

Bob Dylan released his debut album of mostly folk standards, **Bob Dylan**.

1963: When Lesley Gore recorded "It's My Party" she was a junior in high school and fans would show up on her front lawn!

1963 Sixteen-year-old Lesley Gore has her first #1 with **It's My Party** from her debut album **I'll Cry If I Want To** and The Beach Boys got to #3 in May with **Surfin' USA** which went on to become the 'single of the year'.

Peter, Paul and Mary took **Puff the Magic Dragon** to #2 in May but courted controversy when speculation arose that the song contained veiled references to smoking marijuana.

1964 The British Beatles invaded the US this year and won the accolade for most Top Ten hits. **I Want to Hold Your Hand**, (#1), **She Loves You, Please Please Me, Twist and Shout, Can't Buy Me Love**, (#1), **Do You Want to Know a Secret, Love Me Do**, (#1), **P.S. I Love You, A Hard Day's Night**, (#1), **I Feel Fine**, (#1), and **She's a Woman**.

The Supremes have five successive #1 hits, three this year, **Where Did Our Love Go, Baby Love** and **Come See About Me**.

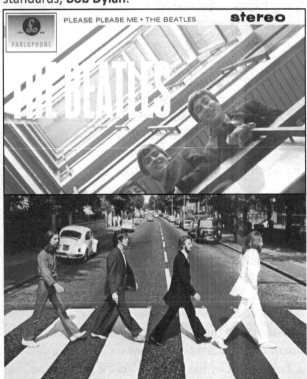

"The Fab Four", John Lennon, Paul McCartney, George Harrison and Ringo Star were the ultimate pop phenomenon of the '60s.

IN THE 1960s

1965 Another great year for British groups, Herman's Hermits have six top ten hits. The Supremes 'fourth in a row #1's' **Stop in the Name of Love** keeps the Hermit's first hit, **Can't You Hear My Heartbeat** (#2) from the top spot.

You've Lost That Lovin' Feelin', written and produced by Phil Spector and sung by the Righteous Brothers, is #1 in February.

1966 California Dreamin' by The Mamas & The Papas is the Top Hot Billboard single of the year and following in her father's footsteps, Nancy Sinatra achieves #1 here and in the UK with **These Boots are Made for Walkin'**.

Good Vibrations sung by The Beach Boys becomes an immediate hit both sides of the Atlantic. It was the most expensive single recorded at that time.

1967 An important year for psychedelic rock and famous for its 'Summer of Love' in San Francisco, however, Aretha Franklin was the star of the Billboard with **I Never Loved a Man**, (#9), **Respect**, (#1), **Baby I Love You**, (#4), **A Natural Woman** (#8) and **Chain of Fools** (#2 Jan '68).

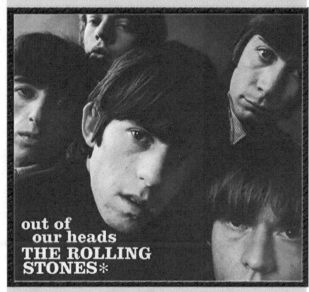

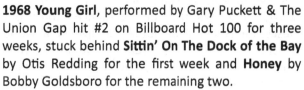

1965: The Rolling Stones have their first #1 US hit with "(I Can't Get No) Satisfaction", followed up by the #1 LP Out of Our Heads.

1968 Young Girl, performed by Gary Puckett & The Union Gap hit #2 on Billboard Hot 100 for three weeks, stuck behind **Sittin' On The Dock of the Bay** by Otis Redding for the first week and **Honey** by Bobby Goldsboro for the remaining two.

Love Child by The Supremes became their 11th #1.

Herb Alpert, known for his trumpet playing as leader of the Tijuana Brass, went to #1 in June with Burt Bacharach's **This Guy's in Love with You.**

1969 Two significant musical events of the year were the **Rolling Stones concert** in Altamont, California, where a fan was stabbed to death by a Hells Angel employed as security and, in marked contrast, the **Woodstock Festival**, where dozens of the most famous performers in the world played together in an atmosphere of peace and love, in front of 500,000 people.

I Heard It Through the Grapevine by Marvin Gaye was released as a single in October 1968, when it went to #1 from December to January this year. This version became the biggest hit single on the Motown label.

43

DANGEROUS URBAN AIR POLLUTION

In 1963 the federal Weather Bureau identified Los Angeles and New York City as the cities most potentially vulnerable to a large-scale lethal smog in the United States. Such smog has the potential to kill as many as 10,000 people, particularly the elderly and those with breathing difficulties.

The 1966, New York City Thanksgiving Day Parade saw the start of the worst smog ever seen in New York and the next day the city asked commuters to avoid driving unless necessary, and apartment buildings to stop incinerating their residents' garbage and turn heating down to 60 °F. New Yorkers went to work in acrid, sour-tasting air that was almost dead calm. Many had headaches that were not due to thanksgiving dinner excess and their throats scratched.

The smog prompted a swift response by the city government, identifying coal-burning power stations, city buses, and apartment building incinerators as significant contributors to air pollution.

In 1962, the UK's Duke of Edinburgh was in New York for the inaugural dinner of the US branch of the World Wildlife Fund, first set up in Zurich in 1961, and warned his audience that our descendants could be forced to live in a world where the only living creature would be man himself -*"always assuming,"* he said, *"that we don't destroy ourselves as well in the meantime."*

In his speech, the Duke described poachers who were threatening extermination of many big game animals in Africa as "killers for profit ... the get-rich-at-any-price mob." African poachers, he said, were killing off the rhinoceros to get its horn for export to China, *"where, for some incomprehensible reason, they seem to think it acts as an aphrodisiac."* The Duke also criticised the status seekers – people "like the eagle chasers". The bald eagle in North America was being chased and killed by people in light aeroplanes who seem to think it smart to own its feathers and claws.

"What is needed, above all now," he said, *"are people all over the world who understand the problem and really care about it. People who have the courage to see that the conservation laws are obeyed."*

DUKE OF EDINBURGH LAUNCHES WORLD WILDLIFE FUND

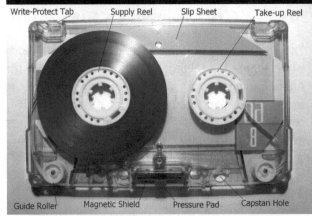

Write-Protect Tab   Supply Reel   Slip Sheet   Take-up Reel

Guide Roller   Magnetic Shield   Pressure Pad   Capstan Hole

THE CASSETTE TAPE

The cassette tape was first developed by Philips in Belgium in 1962. These two small spools inside its plastic case, which wind magnetic-coated film on which the audio content is stored and pass it from one side to the other, meant music could now be recorded and shared by everyone.

Up until now, music was typically recorded on vinyl which needed a record player, or on reel-to-reel recorders which were comparatively expensive and difficult to use and neither of which were portable. The cassette player allowed individuals to record their favorite songs easily and also take their music with them "on-the-go". Music lovers soon learned how to create their own mixed tapes, for themselves or to share with friends.

More than 3 billion tapes were sold between 1962 and 1988.

A DECADE OF INVENTIONS

Many of the things we use today were invented in the Sixties.

Computing was about to move from massive mainframes to desk tops. We had BASIC programming language, the UNIX operating system, the mouse, and DRAM computer memory. Data storage was improved by the invention of the Video Disk and Compact Disc (CD).plus the video game console.

Personal safety clothing and army protection was enhanced by Kevlar which is 5 times as strong as steel but only a fifth of the weight. The Wonderbra was also launched in 1964.

We also invented the weather satellite, bubble wrap, the LED, Valium, Aspartame (the most popular artificial sweetener in the world), the hand held calculator (we now use our phones), and the 911 emergency call number.

The ATM was introduced in 1969. Seemingly simple - you put in your card plus a code and out comes cash - it also allows you to do this from anywhere and any ATM in the world. You bank in Denver but can see your account balance and get a statement in London, Rome, Tokyo - anywhere!

1960 - 1969

1960 Oct: In baseball, Pittsburgh Pirates player Bill Mazeroski becomes the first person to end a **World Series** with a home run.

Dec: In the **NFL Championship**, the Philadelphia Eagles beat the Green Bay Packers 17-13 at Franklin Field in Philadelphia.

1961 Feb: The World Figure Skating Championships in Prague are cancelled after the entire USA team is killed in a plane crash en route to the competition.

Apr: At the basketball **NBA Finals**, Boston Celtics won 4 games to 1 over the St Louis Hawks.

1962 Sept: Sonny Liston knocks out Floyd Patterson after two minutes into the first round to win the **World Heavyweight Championship** in Chicago.

1963 Apr-May: The Pan American Games are held in São Paulo, Brazil. Twenty-two nations took part.

1964 Dec: The Buffalo Bills win 20-7 over the San Diego Chargers in this year's **AFL Championship.**

Oct: The Summer Olympics are held in Tokyo, Japan. The US win the most gold medals (36).

1965 Apr: At the **Masters** in Atlanta, Jack Nicklaus shoots a record 17 under par to win.

1966 Jul: Kansan Jim Ryun sets a new **world record for the mile** at 3min 51.3secs.

1967 Jul: Defending champion Billie Jean King (US) defeats Ann Haydon-Jones (UK) in the **Wimbledon** Women's Singles Championship.

1968 Jun: In golf, Lee Trevino becomes the first golfer to shoot in the 60s in every round of the **US Open**.

1969 Jul: Just hours after Neil Armstrong lands on the moon, Gaylord Perry, **San Francisco's pitcher,** hits the first home run of his career. Some six years previously his manager had quipped, '*They'll put a man on the moon before he hits a home run!*'

1967 AMERICA'S CUP

The 1967 America's Cup was held at Newport, Rhode Island where the US defender 'Intrepid' defeated the Australian challenger 'Dame Pattie' by four races to zero. She had beaten two other American contenders 'Columbia' and 'American Eagle' to become the defender.

The America's Cup was originally called the 'RYS £100 Cup', first awarded in 1851 by the British Royal Yacht Squadron for a race around the Isle of Wight in the UK. A schooner, 'America', owned by a syndicate of members from the New York Yacht Club won and in 1857, they renamed the cup and donated it to the NYYC on condition that it be made available for perpetual international competition.

It is considered the pinnacle of yacht racing and is the oldest trophy in international sport. Every four years, teams compete in yachts that represent the cutting edge of yacht design and technology.

IN THE 1960s

1964 OLYMPIC GAMES

In 1964, the first Olympic Games to be held in Asia, took place in Japan during October to avoid the city's midsummer heat and humidity and the September typhoon season. It marked many milestones in the history of the modern Games; a cinder running track was used for the last time in the athletics events, while a fibreglass pole was used for the first time in the pole-vaulting competition. These Games were also the last occasion that hand timing by stopwatch was used for official timing.

25 world records were broken and 52 of a possible 61 Olympic records were also broken. Ethiopian runner Abebe Bikila won his second consecutive Olympic marathon. Bob Hayes won the men's 100 metres and then anchored the US 400 metre relay team to a world record victory.

The US topped the medal table with 36 golds. Don Schollander won four gold medals in swimming and 15-year-old Sharon Stouder winning four medals in women's swimming, three of them gold.

Peter Snell, winning the 1500 metres.

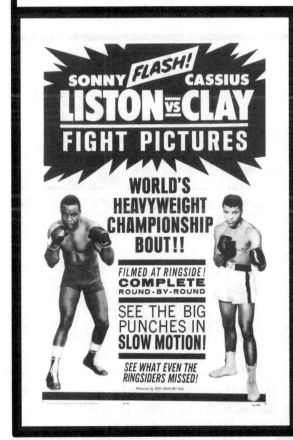

CASSIUS CLAY HEAVYWEIGHT CHAMPION OF THE WORLD

In 1964, Cassius Clay, later this year to be known as Muhammad Ali, fought and gained Sonny Liston's title of Heavyweight Champion of the World. The big fight took place in Miami Beach in February.

Liston was an intimidating fighter and Clay was the 7-1 under-dog, but still he engaged in taunting his opponent during the build-up to the fight, dubbing him *"the big ugly bear"*, stating *"Liston even smells like a bear"* and claiming, *"After I beat him, I'm going to donate him to the zoo!"*
The result of the fight was a major upset as Clay's speed and mobility kept him out of trouble and in the third round hit Liston with a combination that opened a cut under his left eye and eventually, Liston could not come out for the seventh round.
A triumphant Clay rushed to the edge of the ring and, pointing to the ringside press, shouted: *"Eat your words!"* adding the words he was to live up to for the rest of his life, *"I am the greatest!"*

TRANSPORT

STREAMLINERS

This Legendary American Passenger Train was unlike all the trains before, sleek, streamlined and colorful but private railroads watched helplessly as passenger traffic plummeted and cars and planes took over passenger transport in the 60s.

THE PERSONAL JET PACK

The 'jet pack' was developed in the 1960s by the US military to be used as a personal transport device. Propelling the wearer vertically into the air, the technology did not become commercially viable.

BIG TRUCKS

The decline of railroads and improvements in highways and trucks led to a massive growth in road haulage.

CARS OF THE DECADE

Cars were moving beyond a utilitarian form of transport into statements about the owner's status and lifestyle. The Sixties saw the Ford Mustang, the 1966 Pontiac GTO, the Lincoln Continental, the E-type Jaguar and VW Camper Van.

IN THE 1960s

HELLS ANGELS
'HARDASS' OR GALLANT?

By the 60s, the working-class 'folk hero' club, the Hells Angels, were identified by their choice of motorcycles. The Angels rode, eulogised and worshipped Harley-Davidsons, and only Harley-Davidsons.

Restored or rebuilt and polished, the bikes would be 'chopped' to the owner's particular requirements, cutting off fenders, changing handlebars and painting them bright colors.

Hells Angels were well known for rowdy, vulgar, occasionally deviant behavior, BUT - many had a soft spot for stranded motorists or lone women out at night. Angels would be seen at the side of the road helping a driver with his stalled car, and even escorting a lone woman home through the dark, deserted Californian streets.

THE JUMBO JET

The development of the Boeing 747 began in April 1966, with the close co-operation of Pan Am after they requested an airliner two-and-a-half times the size of its existing 707. The carrier placed a 25-aircraft order for the 747 and it became the world's first wide bodied, twin-aisle airliner. This, soon to be called 'the Jumbo Jet', was the first jet designed to include a second deck. This was originally intended to be the full length of the aircraft, but it failed to meet safety requirements for evacuation at the time, and the result was the smaller partial deck. The first aircraft was completed in September 1968 and Pan Am started the regular New York to London service with 350 passengers and 20 crew. This first version of the Jumbo, the 747-100 saw limited success, with only 205 aircraft sold, but it was the next model developed in the early 70s that fully realized its potential.

THE MAJOR NEWS STORIES

1970 - 1974

1970:

Mar: NASA's Explorer 1, the first US satellite re-enters the Earth's atmosphere after 12 years in orbit.

April: The 1970 United States Census begins, and counts 203,392,031 residents.

June: The world's first Pride Parade takes place in Chicago, with another in San Francisco later on the same day.

1971:

Jan: The Public Health Cigarette Act comes into force banning television cigarette advertisements.

Mar: The first Starbucks coffee shop opens in Elliot Bay, Seattle.

1972:

Jun: The 'Watergate' scandal begins in Richard Nixon's administration in the US.

Sep: After the long-awaited chess 'Match of the Century', Bobby Fischer beats Boris Spassky of the Soviet Union to become the first American World Chess Champion.

Sep: Eleven Israeli athletes are murdered by Arab terrorists at the Munich Olympics.

1973:

Jan: The United Kingdom joins the European Economic Community, later to become the EU.

Apr: The first handheld cellular phone call is made by Martin Cooper in New York City. The World Trade Center is opened officially in New York City.

May: Skylab, the USA's first space station is launched

1974:

Aug: Richard Nixon resigns to avoid being removed by impeachment and conviction for his part in the Watergate scandal. Gerald R Ford becomes President.

Dec: Nelson Rockefeller is confirmed as Vice President.

1972: A Japanese soldier who obeyed orders never to surrender, was captured after 28 years of hiding on the Pacific Island of Guam. Sergeant Shoichi Yokoi, now 56, had never heard of either the atomic bomb or television or the jet aircraft he would go home on.

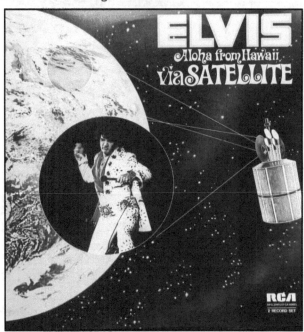

1973: In January, Elvis Presley's concert in Hawaii is the first show by an entertainer to be televised worldwide by satellite and is watched by more people than watched the Apollo Moon landings. In the US, to avoid clashing with Super Bowl VII, it was not aired until April.

1975: The first 'Blockbuster'. Universal Pictures release Steven Spielberg's adaptation of Peter Benchley's bestseller Jaws across the United States. The movie's 25-foot great white shark was played by three full-scale mechanical models towed by submerged 'sleds' or guided by hidden scuba divers. Trouble with these and filming on the ocean, meant filming went way over budget.

1977: 'Snow in Tropical Miami', Florida, for the only time in history, although for the most part the snowflakes melted when they made contact with the ground. That day, temperatures only reached a chilly high of 47degrees and dipped in places into the 30s and caused more than $300 million in agricultural damage in South Florida.

1975 - 1979

1975:
Apr: The Vietnam War ends with the Fall of Saigon to the Communists. South Vietnam surrenders unconditionally.
Sep: President Gerald Ford survives a second assassination attempt, this time in San Francisco.

1976:
Apr: Apple Computer Company is formed in California by Steve Jobs and Steve Wozniak.
Sep: The Viking 2 spacecraft lands at Utopia Planitia on Mars.
Nov: Microsoft is officially registered.
Nov: Jimmy Carter defeats Gerald Ford in the presidential election becoming the first candidate from the Deep South to win since the Civil War.

1977:
Jan: The Commodore PET, the world's first personal computer, is demonstrated in Chicago.
Jan: Jimmy Carter is sworn in as the 39th President of the United States.
Aug: Elvis Presley, king of rock 'n' roll, dies at his home, Gracelands.

1978:
Aug: A state emergency is declared following the revelation that a Niagara Falls neighbourhood is built on a toxic waste dump.
Oct: Pier 39 opens on Fisherman's Wharf, San Francisco.

1979:
Mar: A serious accident occurs at the Three Mile Island nuclear power plant in Pennsylvania.
Nov: 3,000 Iranian radicals, mostly students, invade the U.S. Embassy in Tehran and take 90 hostages (53 of whom are American). They demand that the United States send the former Shah of Iran back to stand trial.

THE HOME

Increasing Comfort and Prosperity

Homes were bright and comfortable in the 1970's. Kitchen and bathroom floors were covered with brightly patterned linoleum, hard wearing and easy to clean up the spills from the kids. Teenagers could lie on the 'impossible to clean', loopy shag pile carpet, or lounge in 'impossible to get out of' bean bag chairs,

watching films on VHS video cassettes or watch live programmes on the family's color television set.

The ubiquitous macramé owl, or plant holder complete with trailing fern, might dangle in the corner adjacent to the bulky, stone faced, rustic fireplace. A crocheted 'granny squares' blanket might be thrown over the back of the floral covered couch, all in a soft light from the fringed shade on the table lamp.

Ready Meals For Kids

TV dinners had been around since the 50's, but it was not until 1971 that Libby's first commercially successful kiddie version arrived.

'Libbyland Dinners', with enticing names like *'Safari Supper', 'Sea Diver's Dinner'* and *'Pirate Picnic'* included the food children liked to eat, hot dogs, hamburgers, fish sticks, etc. plus a 'strictly for the kids' treat like chocolate milk mix. The back of the box had puzzles and games and dressed in a white suit and cowboy hat, 'Libby the Kid' battled constantly with 'Mean Jean' to hold on to his prized dinner!

The bottom of each meal tray had cartoon characters for kids to 'find' which encouraged them to eat everything up!

IN THE 1970s

Teenage Home Entertainment

1978 was the peak year for 8-track sales and lucky teenagers who had a Rec room, often in the basement where the wood panelling might be a bit gloomy, would hang out with friends, listening to Olivia Newton-John, Donna Summer and Neil Diamond.

Meanwhile, the adults, upstairs, still often entertained at home. Meals were inspired by the enormously popular TV shows of Julia Child, 'The French Chef' who was forefront in introducing the concept of healthy eating – and Beef Bourguignon - to the country. Dishes were often cooked and served in the 'all American' colourful, patterned Pyrex dishes and the adventurous melted cheese Fondue party was all the rage. Then to finish it off, 'Watergate Salad', a dessert consisting of a 'salad' of Kraft instant pistachio pudding, canned pineapple, whipped cream, pecans and marshmallows.

The first Starbucks opened in 1971 but most coffee was brewed at home and 'Mr Coffee' simplified the process with his automatic-drip kitchen coffee machine.

1970 - 1974

1970 Garry Trudeau's comic strip 'Doonesbury' is first published in two dozen newspapers across the States.

Jacqueline Kennedy selects Aaron Shikler to provide the posthumous portrait of John F Kennedy to serve as his official White House portrait.

1971 Coco Chanel, the French fashion designer dies. (Born 1883).

The first e-book, a copy of the US Declaration of Independence, is posted on the mainframe computer at the University of Illinois.

1972 Laszlo Toth attacks Michelangelo's 'La Pietà' in St Peter's Basilica (Vatican City) shouting that *he* is Jesus Christ.

Ira Levin's book 'The Stepford Wives' is published. It is made into a film in 1975.

1973 The Supreme Court delivers its decision in the 'Miller v California' case establishing the "Miller Test" for determining obscenity.

Andy Warhol created his portrait of Chinese Communist leader Mao Zedong and in 1975, he published 'The Philosophy of Andy Warhol' in which he expressed his view, 'Making money is art, and working is art and good business is the best art.'

1974 Mikhail Baryshnikov, the 26-year-old star of Leningrad's Kirov Ballet, defects to the West while touring with a Bolshoi company in Toronto.

The Terracotta Army of Qin Shi Huang, thousands of life-size clay models of soldiers, horses and chariots, is discovered at Xi'an in China.

1975 - 1979

1975 Bill Gates and Paul Allen found Microsoft in Albuquerque, New Mexico.

Stephen King's second horror novel 'Salem's Lot' is published. It is nominated for the World Fantasy Award in 1976.

1976 Alex Haley's historical narrative novel 'Roots' was the best-selling novel this year and won a special Pulitzer Prize.

The Jimmy Carter Peanut Statue is erected in Plains, Georgia to support him during the presidential election.

1977 'Annie' is the most successful musical on Broadway this year. The original production runs for 2,377 performances.

Marilyn French publishes her debut novel 'The Women's Room' launching her as a major participant in the feminist movement.

1978 The arcade video game, 'Space Invaders' is released.

The ABC Evening News becomes ABC World News Tonight and employs a unique three-anchor setup from Washington, Chicago and London, England.

1979

The Sony Walkman, portable cassette player is released allowing music to be listened to 'on the move'.

IN THE 1970s

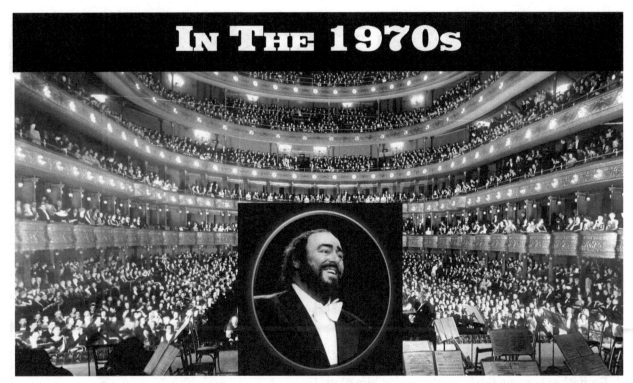

Pavarotti at the Met.

It was in his third season at the Metropolitan Opera House in New York that Luciano Pavarotti, the operatic tenor, would skyrocket to stardom. The company imported Covent Garden's production of Donizetti's *La Fille du Régiment* in 1972 as a vehicle for Joan Sutherland. The great Australian diva enjoyed a huge triumph, but the surprise for the audience was the young Italian tenor by her side who shared an equal part in the phenomenal success. This was the historic first Met performance telecast live on PBS as part of the long-running series that continues to the present day.

The Terracotta Army

'The Qin Tomb Terracotta Warriors and Horses' was constructed between 246-206BC as an afterlife guard for China's First Emperor, Qin Shihuang, from whom, China gets its name. He ordered it built to remember the army he led to triumph over other warring states, and to unite China.

The tomb and the army were all made by hand by some 700,000 artisans and labourers, and comprises thousands of life-size soldiers, each with different facial features and expressions, clothing, hairstyles and gestures, arranged in battle array.

All figures face east, towards the ancient enemies of Qin State, in rectangular formations and three separate vaults include rows of kneeling and standing archers, chariot war configurations and mixed forces of infantry, horse drawn chariots plus numerous soldiers armed with long spears, daggers and halberds.

FILMS

1970 - 1974

1970 Love Story, was the biggest grossing film a sentimental, tearjerker with the often quoted tag line, "Love means never having to say you're sorry." Nominated for the Academy Awards Best Picture, it was beaten by **Patton** which won 7 major titles that year.

1971 The Oscar winner was **The French Connection** with Gene Hackman as a New York police detective, Jimmy 'Popeye' Doyle, chasing down drug smugglers. Hackman was at the peak of his career in the 70's.

1972 Francis Ford Coppola's gangster saga, **The Godfather** became the highest grossing film of its time and helped drive a resurgence in the American film industry.

1973 Three films, **The Exorcist**, **The Sting** and **American Graffit**i grossed over $100 million. The Exorcist won 4 Golden Globe Awards including Best Drama, but it was The Sting that swept the Academy Awards with Best Film, Best Director, Best Screenplay and Best Score.

1974 New films this year included **The Godfather Part II,** which won the Oscar, **Blazing Saddles** the comedy western and the disaster film, **The Towering Inferno** starring Paul Newman and Steve McQueen.

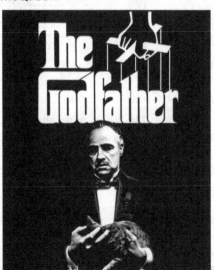

1975 - 1979

1975 One Flew Over the Cuckoo's Nest, an allegorical film set in a mental hospital, starring Jack Nicholson, beat tough competition for Best Picture from Spielberg's **Jaws** and Altman's **Nashville.**

1976 Jodi Foster won an Oscar in Martin Scorsese's gritty film **Taxi Driver** which examines alienation in urban society but it was Sylvester Stallone's **Rocky** that carried off the Best Picture award.

1977 Annie Hall from Woody Allen, the winner of Best Picture is a masterpiece of witty and quotable one-liners.

1978 The Vietnam War is examined through the lives of three friends from a small steel-mill town before, during and after their service in **The Deer Hunter**. A powerful and disturbing film.

1979 In this year's Best Picture, **Kramer v Kramer** there is a restaurant scene where Dustin Hoffman throws his wine glass at the wall. Only the cameraman was forewarned, Meryl Streep's shocked reaction was genuine!

Star Wars

Star Wars all began with George Lucas's spectacular film in 1977. The epic space fantasy, telling the adventures of characters "A long time ago in a galaxy far, far away", and this first film was a world beater in special effects technology using new computerised and digital effects. It rapidly became a phenomenon, Luke Skywalker, Jedi Knights, Princess Leia and Darth Vader becoming household names. An immensely valuable franchise grew up to include the films, television series, video games, books, comics and theme parks which now amounts to billions of dollars and the film introduced the phrase "May the Force be with you" into common usage.

Apocalypse Now

Joseph Conrad's book 'Heart of Darkness' was the inspiration for producer and director Francis Ford Coppola's psychological film, a metaphor for the madness and folly of war itself for a generation of young American men. Beautiful, with symbolic shots showing the confusion, violence and fear of the nightmare of the Vietnam War, much of it was filmed on location in the Philippines where expensive sets were destroyed by severe weather, a typhoon called 'Olga', Marlon Brando showed up on set overweight and completely unprepared and Martin Sheen had a near-fatal heart attack.

This led to the film being two and a half times over budget and taking twice the number of scheduled weeks to shoot. When filming finally finished, the release was postponed several times as Coppola had six hours of film to edit. The helicopter attack scene with the 'Ride of the Valkyries' soundtrack is one of the most memorable film scenes ever.

FASHION

Women Wear the Trousers

It is often said that 1970s styles had no direction and were too prolific. French couture no longer handed down protocol of what we should be wearing, and the emerging street style was inventive, comfortable, practical for women or glamorous. It could be home-made, it was whatever you wanted it to be, and the big new trend was for gender neutral clothes, women wore trousers in every walk of life, trouser suits for the office, jeans at home and colourful, tight-fitting ones for in between. Trouser legs became wider and 'bell-bottoms', flared from the knee down, with bottom leg openings of up to twenty-six inches, made from denim, bright cotton and satin polyester, became mainstream. Increasingly 'low cut', they were teamed with platform soles or high cut boots until they could not flare anymore, and so, by the end of the decade they had gone, skin-tight trousers, in earth tones, greys, whites and blacks were much more in vogue.

And the Hot Pants

In the early 70s, women's styles were very flamboyant with extremely bright colours and, in the winter, long, flowing skirts and trousers *but* come the summer, come the Hot Pants. These extremely short shorts were made of luxury fabrics such as velvet and satin designed for fashionable wear, not the practical equivalents for sports or leisure, and they enjoyed great popularity until falling out of fashion in the middle of the decade. Teamed with skin-tight t-shirts, they were favorites for clubwear and principally worn by women, including Jacqueline Kennedy Onassis, Elizabeth Taylor and Jane Fonda, but they were also worn by some high-profile men, David Bowie, Sammy Davis Jnr and Liberace among them, although the shorts were slightly longer than the women's versions, but still shorter than usual. Chest hair, medallions, sideburns and strangely, tennis headbands, finished the look!

In The 1970s

These Boots Are Made For Walking

Boots were so popular in the early 1970s that even men were getting in on the action. It wasn't uncommon to see a man sporting 2" inch platform boots inspired by John Travolta in Saturday Night Fever. The trend was all about being sexy on the dance floor!

And Punk Was Not to Be Ignored

A rebellion against the conformist, middle America society, dirty, simple clothes – ranging from the T-shirt/jeans/leather jacket Ramones look to the low-class, second-hand "dress" clothes of acts like Television or Patti Smith – were preferred over the expensive or colorful clothing popular in the disco scene.

T-shirts, like other punk clothing items, were often torn on purpose. Other items included leather jackets often with anti society slogans and controversial images.

Safety pins and chains held bits of fabric together. Neck chains were made from padlocks and chain and even razor blades were used as pendants.

Body piercings and studs, beginning with the three-stud earlobe, progressing to the ear outline embedded with ear studs, evolved to pins in eyebrows, cheeks, noses or lips and together with tattoos were the beginning of unisex fashion. All employed by male and female alike to offend. The Punk Rock musical movement began in America with bands such as the New York Dolls and The Stooges.

LEISURE

Saturday Morning TV

In the early 70s, Saturday morning cartoons were a rite of passage for children and some of the best cartoons aired during this time slot and they remain as some of the most beloved and often watched shows today.

Successful shows included: The Sylvester & Tweety Show; Scooby-Doo, Where are You; The Bugs Bunny Show; Woody Woodpecker; Goober and the Ghost Chasers and The Robonic Stooges.

The Tom and Jerry Show, aired in 1975, began as a theatrical cartoon series that ran before movies in theatres and is a series of 161 comedy short films created in 1940 by William Hanna and Joseph Barbera. The shows centre on the rivalry between a cat named Tom and a mouse named Jerry. Tom rarely succeeds in catching Jerry, mainly because of Jerry's cleverness, cunning abilities, and luck.

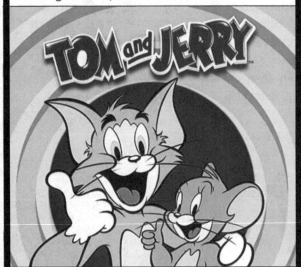

The cartoons use of violence has been criticised in recent years with Tom using axes, hammers, firearms, firecrackers, explosives, traps and poison to kill Jerry. Jerry's methods of retaliation include slicing Tom in half, decapitating him, shutting his head or fingers in a window or a door, tying him to a firework and setting it off, and so on. While Tom and Jerry has often been criticized as excessively violent, there is no blood or gore in any scene.

Saturday Night Fever

Memories of Saturday night and Sunday morning in the discotheque. A mirror ball; strobe lights; 'four on the floor' rhythm; the throb of the bass drum; girls in Spandex tops with hot pants or vividly colored, shiny, Lycra trousers with equally dazzling halter neck tops; boys in imitations of John Travolta's white suit from Saturday Night Fever risking life and limb on towering platform shoes.

These glamorous dancers, clad in glitter, metallic lame and sequins, gyrating as the music pounded out at the direction of the DJ, whirling energetically and glowing bright 'blue-white' under the ultra-violet lights as their owners 'strutted their stuff', perspiration running in rivulets down their backs.

The DJs, stars in their own right, mixed tracks by Donna Summer, the Bee Gees, Gloria Gaynor, Sister Sledge, Chic and Chaka Khan, as their sexy followers, fueled by the night club culture of alcohol and drugs, changed from dancing the Hustle with their partners to the solo freestyle dancing of John Travolta.

IN THE 1970s

Leisure Fads Of The 70s

Every era has its fads and crazes. Think of the Hula Hoop, Frisbee, Pogo Stick and Pet Rock, RISK", 8 track cassette, Walkman, I-Pod - right up to the latest 'apps' enjoyed on the smart phone.

1975: Pet Rock

Advertising executive Gary Dahl was joking around with his friends one night about what would make the perfect pet. He came to the conclusion that a rock would make the perfect pet. One thing led to another, and by the end of 1975, Gary was a millionaire. It's hard to believe people paid good money for a rock. Not a special rock, not a diamond or a gem. Just a regular rock that came with a nest and care booklet. Sure, there were different variations throughout the years, but at the end of the day, it was just a rock.

1978: Lava Lamp

Every student had to have one. Every 'cool' lounge too. A European idea brought to the US by two Americans who set up their factory in Chicago to manufacture the Lava Lite Lamp.

1972: Clackers

Clackers were toys that consisted of two plastic balls connected by a string. The whole point of the toy was that you could wave it around by the handle in the middle and clack the balls together. Surely nothing could go wrong in the hands of children who not just 'clacked' them but also swung them violently against other 'Clackers'?

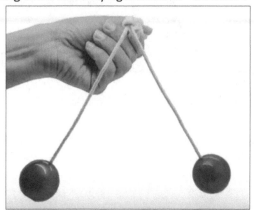

Of course, some balls still shattered and hurt the person holding the toy as well as those around them. Law suits followed. The Clackers craze disappeared as fast as it had started.

1977: CB Radio

Originally used amongst truckers to advise others where the police had speed traps, films such as "Breaker! Breaker!" and "Convoy" helped make CB radios a popular recreational toy amongst many young adults.

MUSIC

1970 - 1974

1970 Number 1 for 3 weeks, **Bridge Over Troubled Water** by Simon and Garfunkel became their 'signature song' selling over 6m copies worldwide. It also became one of the most performed songs of the 20th century, covered by over 50 artists.

1971 Three Dog Night spent 6 weeks at number 1 with "**Joy to the World**" which featured in the film The Big Chill and was also played at the end of every Denver Broncos home victory!
Rod Stewart had 5 weeks at the top spot with **"Maggie May" / "Reason to Believe"** and also topped the charts in the UK, Canada and Australia.

1972 The dominant single was Roberta Flack's **"The First Time Ever I Saw Your Face"** along with the Irish singer Gilbert O'Sullivan whose **"Alone Again (Naturally)"** also topped for 6 weeks.

1973 Roberta Flack's **"Killing Me Softly with His Song"** was number 1 in the US with 5 five weeks at the top and also a chart topper in Canada and Australia.

1974 There were 35 different chart topping records this year including Barbra Streisand, Cher, John Denver (2), Elton John, Paul McCartney, Eric Clapton, Barry White, Olivia Newton-John, Dionne Warwick and Stevie Wonder.

1975 - 1979

1975 Yet another year with 35 different records heading the Billboard Hot 100 charts. The one staying longest was husband-and-wife team were "Captain" Daryl Dragon and Toni Tennille with **"Love Will Keep Us Together"** which won the Grammy Award for Record of the Year.

1976 Elton John and Kiki Dee's duet "**Don't Go Breaking My Heart**" was 4 weeks at number 1, but the best selling record of the year was Rod Stewart's **"Tonight's the Night (Gonna Be Alright)"** with 8 weeks at the top spanning Christmas and the New Year.

1977 The runaway best selling single of the year, staying at the top for 10 weeks was Debby Boone's **"You Light Up My Life"**. Debby, the daughter of singer Pat Boone, won a Grammy Award for Song of the Year, an Academy Award for Best Original Song, and a Golden Globe Award for Best Original Song.

1978 This was the year for the Bee Gees with a combined 12 weeks at the top with **"Stayin' Alive"** (4 weeks) and **"Night Fever"** (8 weeks), which was also the best selling single of the year. Chic, the band founded by Nile Rodgers and bassist Bernard Edwards ended the year at the top with **"Le Freak"**.

1979 The very catchy song **"My Sharona"** by The Knack, had 6 weeks at number 1, in a year with no great stand out hits, although Rod Stewart **"Da Ya Think I'm Sexy?"**, Gloria Gaynor **"I Will Survive"** and Michael Jackson with **"Don't Stop 'til You Get Enough"** all had some time at the top.

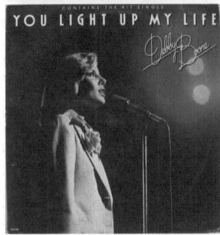

The Decade in Numbers

The **Bee Gees** achieved the most Number 1 songs during the decade (9) and spent the most number of weeks at the top of the chart (27).
You Light Up My Life by Debby Boone (1977) spent the most number of weeks and was the biggest selling US single of the decade.

These acts achieved **four or more Number 1 hits**: Bee Gees (9), Stevie Wonder (5), Eagles (5), Elton John (5), Three Dog Night (4), The Jackson 5 (4), KC and the Sunshine Band (4), John Denver (4), Diana Ross (4), Barbra Streisand (4), Paul McCartney and Wings.
The highest ranked solo female was **Debby Boone**.
The highest ranked solo male was **Rod Stewart**.
The highest ranked group was T**he Bee Gees**.
The four songs with **seven or more weeks at Number 1**. Debby Boone "**You Light Up My Life**" (10 weeks), Bee Gees "**Night Fever**" (8), Rod Stewart "**Tonight's the Night (Gonna Be Alright)**" (8), Andy Gibb "**Shadow Dancing**" (7).

'Danny' and 'Sandy' Fever

Grease, the 1978 musical romantic comedy starring John Travolta (Danny) and Olivia Newton-John (Sandy) had phenomenal success. In June to August 1978, **You're the One That I Want** and in September to October, **Summer Nights**, were a world-wide hit with 1 week at number one in the US but 16 weeks at the top of the UK charts.

Hopelessly Devoted to You was nominated for an Oscar and John Travolta and Olivia Newton-John seemed to be constantly in the public conscience. Critically and commercially successful, the soundtrack album ended 1978 as the second best -selling album in the US, behind the soundtrack of the 1977 blockbuster **Saturday Night Fever,** which also starred John Travolta.

Pocket Calculators

The first pocket calculators came onto the market towards the end of 1970. In the early 70s they were an expensive status symbol but by the middle of the decade, businessmen were quite used to working their sales figures out quickly while 'out of the office'.

Household accounts were made easy and children wished they could use them at school – not just to help with homework. Most early calculators performed only basic addition, subtraction, multiplication and division but the speed and accuracy, sometimes giving up to 12 digit answers, of the machine proved sensational.

In 1972, Hewlett Packard introduced the new, revolutionary HP-35 pocket calculator which as well as the basic operations (add, subtract, multiply and divide) provided a range of advanced mathematical functions.

It was the first scientific, hand-held calculator, able to perform a wide number of logarithmic and trigonometric calculations and also able to store intermediate solutions and utilise scientific notations.

With intense competition, prices of pocket calculators dropped rapidly, and the race was on to produce the smallest possible models. The target was to be no bigger than a credit card.

The Miracle of IVF

In 1971, Patrick Steptoe, gynaecologist, Robert Edwards, biologist, and Jean Purdy, nurse and embryologist set up a small laboratory at the Kershaw's Hospice in Oldham UK, which was to lead to the development of in vitro fertilisation and eventual birth of Louise Brown in 1978.

They developed a technique for retrieving eggs at the right time and fertilising them in the laboratory, believing that they could be implanted back in the uterus. It took more than 80 embryo transfers before the first successful pregnancy, and the birth of Louise, the first 'test-tube baby', heralded the potential happiness of infertile people and a bright future for medical science and technology.

IN THE 1970s

"Houston We Have a Problem"

In April 1970, two days after the launch of Apollo 13, the seventh crewed mission in the Apollo space program and the third meant to land on the Moon, the NASA ground crew heard the now famous message, "Houston, we've had a problem." An oxygen tank had exploded, and the lunar landing was aborted leaving the astronauts in serious danger. The crew looped around the Moon and returned safely to Earth, their safe return being down to the ingenuity under pressure by the crew, commanded by Jim Lovell, together with the flight controllers and mission control. The crew experienced great hardship, caused by limited power, a chilly and wet cabin and a shortage of drinking water.

Even so, Apollo 13 set a spaceflight record for the furthest humans have travelled from Earth.

Tens of millions of viewers watched Apollo 13 splashdown in the South Pacific Ocean and the recovery by USS Iwo Jima.

The global campaigning network **Greenpeace** was founded in 1971 by Irving and Dorothy Stowe, environmental activists. The network now has 26 independent national or regional organisations in 55 countries worldwide.

Their stated goal is to ensure the ability of the earth to nurture life in all its diversity. To achieve this they "use non-violent, creative confrontation to expose global environmental problems, and develop solutions for a green and peaceful future". In detail to:

- Stop the planet from warming beyond 1.5° in order to prevent the most catastrophic impacts of the climate breakdown.
- Protect biodiversity in all its forms.
- Slow the volume of hyper-consumption and learn to live within our means.
- Promote renewable energy as a solution that can power the world.
- Nurture peace, global disarmament and non-violence.

SPORT

1970 A double tragedy when half of the Wichita State University football team die in an October plane crash followed by another crash in November killing 37 players of the Marshall University team.

1971 In the **Super Bowl** Baltimore Colts (AFC) won 16–13 over the Dallas Cowboys (NFC).
Jack Nicklaus wins his ninth major at the **PGA Championship**, the first golfer ever to win all four majors for the second time.

1972 The **Olympic Games** held in Munich are overshadowed by the murder of eleven Israeli athletes and coaches by Palestinian Black September members.

1973 George Foreman knocks out Joe Frazier in only two rounds to take the **World Heavyweight Boxing** Championship title.

1974 Jimmy Connors, the 'bad boy' of tennis, won the **US Open** and also the Australian and British Championships.
The New York Yacht Club retains the **America's Cup** as Courageous defeats Australian challenger Southern Cross, of the Royal Perth Yacht Club.

1975 Muhammad Ali defeats Joe Frazier in the 'Thrilla In Manilla' to maintain the **Boxing Heavyweight Championship** of the world.

1976 The **Summer Olympics** are held in Montreal and the **Winter Olympics** take place in Innsbruck, Austria.
In both games, USSR won most gold medals and most medals overall.
The US came third in both games (10 medals with 3 gold in winter) and 94 medals with 34 gold in summer.

1977 In the **World Figure Skating Championships**, our Linda Fratianne became Ladies' champion.
Tom Watson won the **Augusta Masters** beating Jack Nicklaus by 2 strokes. Later in the year he won the British Open by 1 stroke, again with Jack Nicklaus second.

1978 The **Super Bowl** was won by the Dallas Cowboys (NFC) 27–10 over the Denver Broncos (AFC).
In **World Series Baseball**, New York Yankees win 4 games to 2 over the Los Angeles Dodgers.
In the **World Figure Skating Championships** the Men's champion was Charles Tickner, US.

1978 In Las Vegas, Larry Holmes retains his **World Heavyweight** title with an 11th-round TKO of Earnie Shavers and also in Vegas, Sugar Ray Leonard wins his first world title, beating **WBC World Welterweight** champion Wilfred Benítez by knockout in round 15.

IN THE 1970s

Traffic Lights and Soccer

Before the introduction of Red and Yellow Cards in soccer, cautions or sending a player off had to be dealt with orally, and the language barrier could sometimes present problems.

In the 1966 World Cup, the German referee tried to send Argentinian player Antonio Rattin off the field, but Rattin did not 'want' to understand and eventually was escorted off the pitch by the police! Ken Aston, Head of World Cup Referees, was tasked with solving this problem and the idea of the red and yellow cards came to him when he was stopped in his car at traffic lights. They were tested in the 1968 Olympics and the 1970 World Cup in Mexico and introduced to European leagues soon after.

In 1976, the first player to be sent off using a red card was Blackburn Rovers winger David Wagstaffe.

The Iditarod

The Iditarod, is an annual long-distance sled dog race run in early March. It travels from Anchorage to Nome, entirely within the state of Alaska. Mushers and a team of between 12 and 14 dogs, of which at least 5 must be on the towline at the finish line, cover the distance in 8–15 days or more.

The Iditarod began in 1973 as an event to test the best sled dog mushers and teams but evolved into today's highly competitive race.

1979 Daytona 500

The 1979 Daytona 500 was the first 500-mile race to be broadcast in its entirety live on national television in the United States. The race introduced two new innovative uses of TV cameras, the "in-car" camera and the low angle "speed shot", which are now considered standard in all telecasts of auto racing.

On the final lap, race leaders Cale Yarborough and Donnie Allison collided with each other on the Daytona International Speedway's backstretch. Both drivers' races ended in Daytona's grass infield. The wreck allowed Richard Petty, then over one-half lap behind both, to claim his sixth Daytona 500 win.

As Petty made his way to Victory Lane to celebrate, a fight erupted between Yarborough, Donnie Allison and his brother, Bobby, at the site of the backstretch wreck. Both events were caught by television cameras and broadcast live.

The story made the front page of The New York Times Sports section. NASCAR had arrived as a national sport and began to expand from its southeastern United States base and become a national sport, shedding its moonshine running roots along the way.

Richard Petty and his winning car.

ICONIC MACHINES OF THE DECADE

The Jumbo Jet
Entered service with Pan Am on January 22, 1970. The 747 was the first airplane dubbed a "Jumbo Jet", the first wide-body airliner.

In 1974 Cadillac launched the Fleetwood Sixty Seven Brougham Talisman. This Cadillac was the most elegant car of its era and is a very luxurious classic.

By the 70s imports accounted for over 1 million cars and nearly 20% of cars sold. While the BMW 3 Series didn't come stateside until 1977, sales in the US now account for 30% of all BMW's sales.

The 70s weren't just a time of evolving fashions and styles; it was a time when cars were getting sleeker and more powerful. The Oldsmobile Cutlass was one of the very best selling cars due to its powerful engine, a low price, a roomy interior and a stylish body.

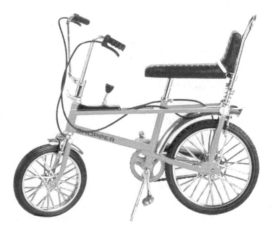

Stylish bicycles boomed in the 1970s and the 'Chopper' bike appeared in many films of the era - usually ridden by a newspaper delivery teenager.
These were not fast or even very comfortable machines, but they had all important 'style'.

In The 1970s

Women Drivers

Bonnie Tiburzi became the first female pilot for American Airlines and the first female pilot for a major American commercial airline. She flew as a Captain on the Boeing 727, Boeing 757 and the Boeing 767.

Janet Guthrie, originally an aerospace engineer, was the first woman to compete in both the Indianapolis 500 and the Daytona 500, both in 1977 and had two class wins in the famed 12 Hours of Sebring endurance race.

Janet Guthrie's 1978 Indy 500 car.

Christine Gonzalez gained nationwide fame in the 1970s as the first woman in the United States to become an engineer for a Class 1 railroad the Santa Fe Railroads. She recalled working back-breaking 12-hours days, seven days a week, along the railroad from El Paso to Albuquerque. She first worked as an engine hostler, moving locomotives around service facilities. Then she learned how to operate a locomotive.

Concorde

The Anglo-French supersonic passenger airliner had a take-off speed of 220 knots (250mph) and a cruising speed of 1350mph – more than twice the speed of sound. With seating for 92 to 128 passengers, Concorde entered service in 1976 and operated for 27 years.

Twenty aircraft were built in total, including six prototypes and in the end, only Air France and British Airways purchased and flew them, due in great part to supersonic flights being restricted to ocean-crossing routes, to prevent sonic boom disturbance over land and populated areas. Concorde flew regular transatlantic flights from London and Paris to New York, Washington, Dulles in Virginia and Barbados and the BA Concorde made just under 50,000 flights and flew more than 2.5m passengers supersonically.

A typical London to New York crossing would take a little less than three and a half hours as opposed to about eight hours for a subsonic flight.

The aircraft was retired in 2003, three years after the crash of an Air France flight in which all passengers and crew were killed.

THE MAJOR NEWS STORIES

1980 - 1984

1980:

May: Mount St. Helens experiences a huge eruption that creates avalanches, explosions, large ash clouds, mudslides, and massive damage. 57 people are killed.

Dec: John Lennon, the former Beatle, age 40, is shot and killed by an obsessed fan in Manhattan.

1981:

March: U.S. President Ronald Reagan survives being shot in the chest outside a Washington, D.C. hotel by John Hinckley, Jr.
July: Prince Charles marries Lady Diana Spencer at St Paul's Cathedral.
Dec: The first American test-tube baby, Elizabeth Jordan Carr, is born in Norfolk, Virginia.

1982:

Jan: Air Florida Flight 90 crashes into the 14th Street Bridge in Washington, D.C., then falls into the Potomac River, killing 78 people.
Apr: Argentina invades the Falkland Islands and the UK retakes possession of them by the end of June.

1983:

Apr: The Space Shuttle Challenger is launched on its maiden voyage
Nov: The U.S. sends nuclear cruise missiles to Greenham Common in Berkshire, England to deter the Soviets.

1984:

Feb: Astronauts Bruce McCandless II and Robert L. Stewart make the first untethered space walk.
Oct: Monterey Bay Aquarium is opened.
Nov: In the United States presidential election the incumbent Republican President Ronald Reagan has a landslide victory and George Bush became Vice President.

1980: Mount St. Helens before and after the eruption. The top third of the mountain was blown away.

1982: EPCOT opened at Disney World in Florida, "...an experimental prototype community of tomorrow that will take its cue from the new ideas and technologies that are now emerging ... a showcase of the ingenuity and imagination of American free enterprise." - *Walt Disney*

1984: On 31 October, Indira Gandhi, Prime Minister of India, was killed by her Sikh bodyguards.
The assassination sparked four days of riots that left more than 8,000 Indian Sikhs dead in revenge attacks.

OF THE 1980s

1985 - 1989

1985: May 31 – Forty-four tornadoes hit Ohio, Pennsylvania, New York and Ontario, including a rare powerful F5. In total, the event killed 90 people.

This extremely violent tornado began in eastern Ohio, and tore directly through the towns of Niles, Ohio and Wheatland, Pennsylvania, producing F5 damage at both locations.

The tornado killed 18 people and injured 310, and was the most violent and deadly of the 44 recorded that day. Registering F5 on the Fujita scale, it remains the only F5 in Pennsylvania history, and was also the most violent tornado reported in the United States in 1985.

1985:

Jan: The Internet's Domain Name System is created and the country code top-level domain .com is added, the 'com' standing for 'commercial'.

Nov: Microsoft Corporation releases the first international release of Windows 1.0.

1986:

Apr: A Soviet Nuclear reactor at Chernobyl explodes causing the release of radioactive material across much of Europe.

1987:

April: The Simpsons cartoon first appears as a series

Oct: Black Monday: Wall Street crashed by over 20%, the largest one day fall in its history.

1988:

Dec: Suspected Libyan terrorist bomb explodes on Pan Am jet over Lockerbie in Scotland on December 21st killing all 259 on board and 11 on the ground.

1989:

June: In Beijing's Tiananmen Square an unknown Chinese protester, "Tank Man", stands in front of a column of military tanks

1989: March 24 - The Exxon Valdez ran aground on Bligh Reef in Prince William Sound, Alaska, spilling its cargo of crude oil into the sea which resulted in massive damage to the environment, including the killing of around 250,000 seabirds, nearly 3,000 sea otters, 300 harbour seals, 250 bald eagles and up to 22 killer whales.

It is considered to be one of the worst human-caused environmental disasters. The Valdez spill is the second largest in US waters, after the 2010 Deepwater Horizon oil spill, in terms of volume released. The oil, originally extracted at the Prudhoe Bay Oil Field, eventually impacted 1,300 miles (2,100 km) of coastline.

Nov: The Fall of the Berlin Wall heralds the end of the Cold War and communism in East and Central Europe.

71

THE HOME

A Busier Life

In the 1980's, life became more stressful, there were two recessions, divorce rates were increasing, women were exercising their rights and these years were the beginning of the end of the traditional family unit. With single parent families or both parents at work and a generally 'busier' life, there was a fundamental change to the family and home. There was also a lot more choice.

Many more 'lower cost' restaurants, chilled ready-made meals, instant foods such as the meaty McRib, first brought out in 1981, Hot Pockets the savoury pastries with fillings such as Ham & Cheddar and Pepperoni Pizza. Together with the boom in electrical labour-saving devices from food processors and microwaves to dishwashers and automatic washing machines, sandwich toasters and jug kettles, all added up to more free time from housework and cooking.

Home Décor

Flower patterns were all the rage in early 1980s home décor, from flower patterned upholstery and drapes to floral wallpapers. Drapes were floor-sweeping, featuring all the bells and whistles, such as valances, swag and tails and ornate tiebacks.

While virtually any floral bedding was a hit at the time, Laura Ashley's frilly, girly collection was particularly popular among the era's more fashionable home designers for comforters, linens and curtains and could even be used for the chic 'over-bed' canopy while side tables were never fully dressed without a floor-length ruffled skirt and protective glass topper.

The Telephone Answering Machine

There once was a time when, to use a telephone, both people had to be on the phone at the same time. You had to pick up the phone when it rang. The answering machine, one cassette tape for the outgoing message and one to record incoming calls, changed all that. By allowing people to take calls when they were away and respond to any message at a later time.

Children's Playtime

For children, toys of the early 80s had a bit of a 70s feel, Star Wars action figures, remote controlled cars and trucks, Barbie dolls and Action Men, but by 1983 there was a huge increase in toys like Transformers, Care Bears, a large number of talking robot toys, My Little Pony, Teenage Mutant Ninja Turtles and Cabbage Patch Kids which was THE craze of 1983 – these odd looking 'little people' were the first images to feature on disposable 'designer' nappies! Rubik's Cube was very popular too.

Basic Atari video games evolved to Nintendo's NES game system and all of them competed with Apple and Sinclair home computers and personal Walkman stereos.

ART AND CULTURE

1980 - 1984

1980 "Who shot J.R.?" was an advertising catchphrase that CBS created to promote their TV show, 'Dallas', referring to the cliff hanger of the finale of the previous season. The episode, 'Who Done It?' aired in November with an estimated 83 million viewers tuning in.

1981 Guernica the large 1937 oil painting by Spanish artist Pablo Picasso is one of his best-known works, regarded by many art critics as the most moving and powerful anti-war painting in history, was returned from New York to Madrid.

1982 MTV was successful and music videos began to have a larger effect on the record industry. Pop artists such as Michael Jackson, Whitney Houston, Duran Duran, Prince, Cyndi Lauper and Madonna mastered the format and helped turn this new product into a profitable business.

1983 Leonard Bernstein's **A Quiet Place**, his last opera, opens in Houston. It has been jointly commissioned by the Kennedy Center, the Houston Grand Opera and La Scala.

1984 Motown singer Marvin Gaye was shot dead by his father at his home in Los Angeles on April 1, 1984, the day before his 45th birthday

1985 - 1989

1985 'Live Aid' pop concerts in London and Philadelphia raise over £50,000,000 for famine relief in Ethiopia.

Nintendo finally decided in 1985 to release its Famicom (released in 1983 in Japan) in the United States under the name Nintendo Entertainment System (NES). It was bundled with Super Mario Bros. and it suddenly became a success.

1986 Chess is a musical whose story involves a politically driven, Cold War–era chess tournament between two grandmasters from America and the USSR and their fight over a woman who manages one and falls in love with the other. Inspiration was from the battle between American grandmaster Bobby Fischer, and Russian Grandmaster Anatoly Karpov.

1987 'The Simpsons' cartoon first appears as a series of animated short films on the 'Tracey Ullman Show'.

1988 Salman Rushdie published 'The Satanic Verses' a work of fiction which caused a widespread controversy and forced Rushdie to live in hiding out of fear for his life.

1989 May – Tiananmen Square protests of 1989: The sculpture Goddess of Democracy constructed by students of the China Central Academy of Fine Arts from extruded polystyrene foam, is unveiled. Four days later it is toppled by a Chinese Army tank.

IN THE 1980s

The Great Musical Revival

By the start of the 1980's, the Broadway Theatres were facing rising costs and falling audiences and fought to be saved from demolition. – until the revival of the Musical, led by Andrew Lloyd Webber.

In 1981, his first 'unlikely' musical **Cats** led by Elaine Paige, went on to be the first 'megamusical' spectacular on Broadway and in London's West End.

It was followed in 1984 by **Starlight Express.**

In 1986, the **Phantom of the Opera** opened to overwhelmingly positive reviews and in 2006 it overtook Lloyd Webber's Cats as the longest running show on Broadway.

In 1987 **Les Misérables** brought the Royal Shakespeare Company 's expertise in high drama to the musical which was set amidst the French Revolution and brought fame to its writers, Alain Boubill and Claude-Michel Schönberg fame and producer Cameron Mackintosh his millions.

Other hit musicals of the decade include:
Grease II
The Blues Brothers
Fame
Xanadu
The Best Little Whorehouse in Texas.

1980 - 1984

1980 The epic **The Empire Strikes Back** is released and is the highest-grossing film of the year, just as its predecessor, **Star Wars** was in 1977. However, the Oscar for Best Picture went to **Ordinary People**, the psychological drama depicting the disintegration of an upper middle-class family in Illinois.

1981 Chariots of Fire based on the true story of two British athletes, one Christian, one Jewish, in the 1924 Olympics, won the Academy Awards.
The film's title was inspired by the line "Bring me my Chariot of fire!" from Blake's poem adapted as the hymn 'Jerusalem'.

1982 Spielberg's science fiction film of **ET the Extra Terrestrial** was a huge box office hit this year, the scene when the little green extra-terrestrial learns to speak, instilled "ET phone home" into the collective memory. The rather more down to earth biographical film of Mahatma Gandhi **Gandhi**, picked up the Best Film award.

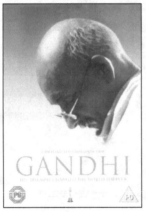

1983 Terms of Endearment won 5 Oscars and was the second highest grossing film behind **Star Wars: Episode VI – Return of the Jedi** staring Mark Hamill as Luke Skywalker, Harrison Ford as Han Solo, and Carrie Fisher as Leia Organa, who is a leader of the Rebellion, Luke's twin sister, and Han's love interest.

1984 Amadeus the fictionalised story of the composer Wolfgang Amadeus Mozart and a supposed rivalry with Italian composer Antonio Salieri, featuring much of Mozart's music, won the imagination of the audiences and the Best Film of the Year award too.

1985 - 1989

1985 Spielberg's 'coming of age' epic starring Whoopi Goldberg in her breakthrough role, **The Color Purple**, was nominated for eleven Academy Awards but failed to achieve a single win. The prize went to Meryl Streep and Robert Redford in the romantic drama, **Out of Africa.**

1986 The first of Oliver Stone's trilogy based on his experiences in the Vietnam war, **Platoon** picks up this year's Oscar for Best Film, beating two British nominations, **A Room with a View** and **The Mission.** This was also the year of the Australian box office runaway success, **Crocodile Dundee.**

1987 The thriller **Fatal Attraction** attracted both favorable reviews and controversy. It put the phrase 'bunny boiler' into the urban dictionary.

1988 Glenn Close was nominated for Best Actress for her role as the Marquise de Merteuil who plots revenge against her ex-lover, in **Dangerous Liaisons.** Dustin Hoffman and Tom Cruise starred in **Rainman**, the winner of Best Film of the year.

1989 Unusually, it was a PG rated film, **Driving Miss Daisy,** that won the Academy Award this year, a gentle, heartwarming comedy which had the serious themes of racism and anti-semitism at its heart. Jessica Tandy at age 81, won Best Actress, the oldest winner to do so.

IN THE 1980s

Steven Spielberg

The 1980s saw the release of several films by Spielberg including **E.T. the Extra-Terrestrial** (1982) and the **Indiana Jones** original trilogy (1981–89). Spielberg subsequently explored drama in the acclaimed **The Color Purple** (1985) and **Empire of the Sun** (1987).

E.T. premiered at the 1982 Cannes Film Festival to an ecstatic reaction. A special screening was organized for President Reagan and his wife Nancy, who were emotional by the end of the film.

He is a major figure of the New Hollywood era and pioneer of the modern blockbuster and the most commercially successful director of all time. A recipient of various accolades, including three Academy Awards, two BAFTA Awards, and four Directors Guild of America Awards, as well as many others.

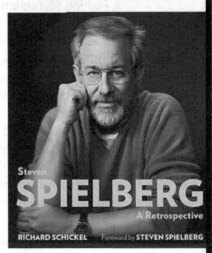

Also in 1984, the Brit David Puttnam produced **The Killing Fields**, a harrowing biographical drama about the Khmer Rouge in Cambodia, based on the experiences of a Cambodian journalist and an American journalist. This film received seven Oscar nominations and won three, most notably Best Supporting Actor for Haing S. Ngor who had no previous acting experience.

Puttnam's career spanned the 1960s to the 1990s and his films have won 10 Oscars, 31 BAFTAs, 13 Golden Globes, nine Emmys, four David di Donatellos in Italy and the Palme d'Or at Cannes.

FASHION

A Fashion Statement

The mid to late 80s was the time to 'make a statement'. The mass media took over fashion trends completely and fashion magazines, TV shows and music videos all played a part in dictating the latest bold fashions.

There was a huge emphasis on bright colours, huge shoulder pads, power suits which gave an exaggerated silhouette like an upside-down triangle, flashy skirts and spandex leggings, velour, leg warmers and voluminous parachute pants.

We wore iconic oversized plastic hoop earrings, rubber bracelets and shiny chain necklaces and huge sunglasses giving faces the appearance of large flies. Men and women alike made their hair 'big' with or without the ubiquitous teased perm and for the girls, glossy pink lips, overly filled-in brows, rainbow-coloured eye-shadows and exaggerated blusher were on trend.

Men too joined in with style and sported oversized blazers with shiny buttons, pinstripe two-piece suits and sweaters, preferably from Ralph Lauren, draped over the shoulders.

Polka Dots

Although not new to the 80s - Disney's Minnie Mouse was first seen in the 1920's wearing the red and white dottie print - polka dots were also very popular.

Bands such as The Beat used them in their music videos and well-known celebrities including Madonna and Princess Diana loved the cool look of polka dot dresses and tops.

When teamed with the oversized earrings of the decade and big hair, while bucking the trend for bright, gaudy colours, they still "made a statement".

Carolina Herrera used polka dots on most of her dresses during the late 1980s and early 1990s and it remains a key print in her collections, a classic.

As Marc Jacobs, the American designer famously said, "There is never a wrong time for a polka dot."

IN THE 1980s

Idols and Jeans

Pale blue, distressed jeans were the fashionable 'street wear', worn semi fitted and held with a statement belt at the natural waistline.

The punk movement had embraced ripped jeans in the '70's and the Sex Pistols brought them into fashion. Teens up and down the country enthusiastically took the scissors to their own jeans, and ripped, frayed or shredded them.

Pop Fashion
If you were into pop music in the 1980s, there's no doubt that superstars Madonna and Wham! influenced what you wore.

Feet also presented a branding opportunity, Patrick Cox had celebrities make his loafers universally desired, and, often credited with kicking off the whole fashion sneaker movement, Nike Air 'Jordans' – named after basketball star, Michael Jordan – were launched in 1985. If you couldn't have them, then high-top Reebok sneakers were also the pinnacle of style -- as were Adidas Superstar kicks and matching tracksuits.

LEISURE

The Fitness Craze

The 1980's had a fitness craze. Celebrities made aerobics videos and endorsed weight loss products and equipment. Health Clubs and Gyms became the place to be and to be seen but were predominantly for men so for women who wanted to exercise in the privacy of their own home, by the mid '80s, there were very few households that didn't own at least one well-worn VHS copy of **'Jane Fonda's Workout'**.

Her 1982 video sold more than 17 million copies, with the actress wearing a striped and belted leotard, violet leggings and leg warmers, big, big hair and in full make-up and working up a sweat to some heavy synth music, inspired a whole generation.

20 Minute Workout was a Canadian-produced aerobics-based television program that ran from 1983 to 1984, in which "a bevy of beautiful girls" demonstrated exercise on a rotating platform.

In the United States, it was syndicated by Orion Television.

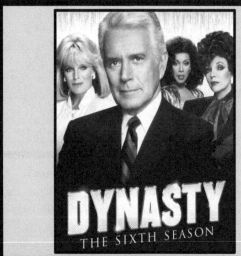

What's On Television?

Television was a very large part of leisure in the 1980s and with the massive growth in video recorders, the whole family had more control over what they watched and when they watched it.

It was the decade when the huge 'soaps' **Dallas** and **Dynasty** dominated the ratings and influenced popular debate as well as fashions. , **'Who Shot JR'** in Dallas watched by 80 million, the finale of **MASH**, 'Goodbye, Farewell and Amen', by more than 100 million.

The **A-Team** action adventure series featured Mr. T and their very cool, black vehicle ran from 1983 to 1987.

Female crime investigators featured through the 1980s with **Cagney & Lacey** running for seven seasons from 1981 to 1988. The series was set in a fictionalized version of Manhattan's 14th Precinct. **Charlie's Angels** were three women who worked for a private investigation agency, and was one of the first shows to show women in roles traditionally reserved for men.

What Was New?

Whilst the 80s made huge advances in technology for leisure, Game Boy and Nintendo, VCRs and CDs, disposable cameras and brick shaped mobile phones too, there were other innovations.

In this decade of high disposable income and the first credit cards, we were spending on BMX bikes, Trivial Pursuit and Rubik's Cubes.

Nike told us to 'Just Do It' and we wondered how we'd ever managed without Post-It Notes and disposable contact lenses.

What the world did not want however, was New Coke. Coca Cola changed their classic formula for a sweeter one which received an extremely poor response.

It was one of the worst marketing blunders ever because for the public, this tampered recipe 'Just wasn't it!'. The company brought back the original Coke and sold this new formula as the 'New Coke' till the early 90s.

MUSIC

1980 - 1984

1980 Abba had their first hit of the year with **Winner Takes it All** followed in November with **Super Trouper.**

Blondie had 6 weeks at number 1 with **Call Me** which was the theme to the 1980 film American Gigolo.

1981 "**Physical**" by Olivia Newton-John was an immediate smash hit, shipping two million copies and spending 10 weeks at number one on the Billboard Hot 100. This was her biggest hit and cemented her legacy as a pop superstar

1982 "**Ebony and Ivory**" by Paul McCartney featuring Stevie Wonder aligns the black and white keys of a piano keyboard with the theme of racial harmony. The single reached number one on both the UK and the US charts .

1983 "**Every Breath You Take**" by the English rock band the Police was the biggest US and Canadian hit of 1983, topping the chart for eight weeks. At the 26th Annual Grammy Awards, the song was nominated for three Grammy Awards,

1984 "**Like a Virgin**" by Madonna was her first number-one in the US. It has sold over six million copies worldwide reaching number one in over 10 countries. The track has also been credited with encouraging women and female performers from the time to embrace their sexuality.

1985 - 1989

1985 "**We Are the World**" is a charity single originally recorded by the supergroup USA for Africa in 1985. It was written by Michael Jackson and Lionel Richie and sold over 20 million copies becoming the eighth-bestselling and fastest selling, physical single of all time.

1986 "**Walk Like an Egyptian**" by the Bangles was the band's first number-one single and the joint longest at number one with "**That's What Friends Are For**" by "Dionne Warwick & Friends", a charity single for AIDS research, winning the Grammy Awards for Best Pop Performance by a Duo or Group with Vocals and Song of the Year. It raised more than $3 million for its cause.

1987 "**Faith**" written and performed by George Michael, held the number-one position for four weeks and, according to Billboard magazine, was the US single of the year.

1988 "**Roll with It**" by Steve Winwood was 4 weeks at number one but Whitney Houston's "**Where Do Broken Hearts Go**" became her seventh consecutive number-one single in the United States—a record that still stands to this day.

1989 "**Miss You Much**" by Janet Jackson and was the second best-selling single of the year behind "**Another Day in Paradise**" by Phil Collins.

Charity Fund Raisers

The 80's saw many records where the proceeds went to charity. Many were prompted by the massive famine in Ethiopia which killed millions of children in the first half of the decade.

The widespread famine in Ethiopia from 1983 to 1985 was the worst famine to hit the country in a century, affecting 8 million people. Almost 200,000 children were orphaned.

Although officially ascribed to drought, it is clear that many deaths and much of the starvation was, at least in part, created by the government's military attacks on so called rebels in the north.

In 1985 the biggest charity record was by USA for Africa the name under which 47 predominantly U.S. artists, led by Michael Jackson and Lionel Richie, recorded the hit single "**We Are the World**". David Bowie and Mick Jagger performed "**Dancing in The Street**" for Ethiopian Famine Relief and it reached number 7 in the US charts. Dionne Warwick, Stevie Wonder, Gladys Knight and Elton John had a number 1 hit with "**That's What Friends Are For**" in support of the American Foundation for AIDS Research.

In 1986 AUA (Artistas Unidos da América) got to number 3 with "**Amor & Paz**" in aid of famine and poverty around the world, and in 1988 Michael Jackson reached number 1 with "**Man in the Mirror**" and "**Another Part of Me**" both of which supported his own Michael Jackson Burn Center, Childhelp and United Negro College Fund.

The biggest charity record in Europe was by Band Aid, the collective name of a charity supergroup featuring mainly British and Irish musicians and recording artists. It was founded in 1984 by Bob Geldof and Midge Ure to raise money for anti-famine efforts in Ethiopia by releasing the song "**Do They Know It's Christmas?**"

This record has become a standard air play number of every Christmas since.

The Compact Disc

At the end of the 70's, Philips and Sony had teamed up to begin working on CDs for the public and decided on a thin, shiny and circular storage disc, which could hold about 80 minutes of music. The disc had a diameter of 120mm, Sony having insisted that the longest musical performance, Beethoven's entire 9th Symphony at 74 minutes, should fit. A CD could hold an immense amount of data, much more than the vinyl record or the cassette and was perfectly portable.

In 2004, worldwide sales of audio CDs, CD-ROMs, and CD-Rs reached about 30 billion discs. In 2007 on the 25th anniversary of its first public release in 1982, it was estimated that 200 billion CDs had been sold worldwide.

The first commercial CD to be pressed was **Visitors** by Abba, followed quickly by the first album, Billy Joel's **52nd Street**. The biggest selling CD of all time is the Eagles 1976 **Their Greatest Hits** album, which has sold over 38 million copies.

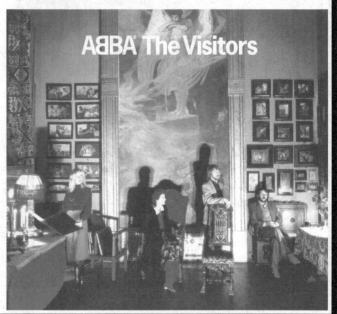

UFOs in the Florida

On Wednesday November 11, 1987, Ed Walters, said that he had been immobilized "*briefly by a blue beam*" and took five photos of the object hovering about 200 feet up in the sky outside his Gulf Breeze home. He described it as being '*right out of a Spielberg movie*'. He claimed that over time and multiple visits he videotaped the UFO and took 32 photographs of it.

Walters or his family reported 19 sightings or encounters. On May 1, 1988, Walters said he felt the presence and saw the UFO and took a photo of it, then "lost consciousness for an hour". He also said that the UFO leaked some kind of liquid that continued to boil even 19 days after he captured it.

Experts poured over the photos and the testimony but it should be noted that the massive Eglin Air Force base is only a short distance away!

In The 1980s

Mount St Helens

In March 1980 a series of volcanic explosions began at Mount St Helens, Washington culminating in a major explosive eruption on May 18. The eruption column rose 80,000 feet (15 miles) into the atmosphere and deposited ash over 11 states and into some Canadian provinces. At the same time, snow, ice, and entire glaciers on the volcano melted, forming a series of large volcanic mudslides that reached as far as 50 miles to the southwest. Thermal energy released during the eruption was equal to 26 megatons of TNT.

Regarded as the most significant and disastrous volcanic eruption in the country's history, about 57 people were killed, hundreds of square miles were reduced to wasteland, thousands of animals were killed, and Mount St. Helens was left with a crater on its north side. The area is now preserved as the Mount St Helens National Volcanic Monument.

One day before the eruption and several months afterwards. About a third of the mountain was blown away.

1980 - 1984

1980 Eight days after the **Boston marathon**, Rosie Ruiz, a Cuban American, is disqualified as the winner 'in the fastest time ever run by a woman'. Investigations found that she did not run the entire course, joining about a half-mile before the finish.

Larry Holmes defeats Muhammed Ali to retain boxing's **WBC World Heavyweight** title. It is Ali's last world title bout.

1981 At **Wimbledon**, John McEnroe defeats Björn Borg to gain his 3rd career Grand Slam title and his 1st Wimbledon title.

In the ladies' final, Chris Evert Lloyd defeats Hana Mandlíková to gain her 12th career Grand Slam title and her third and last Wimbledon title.

1982 In June, at Pebble Beach, the American Tom Watson wins **The US Open** and a month later, at Royal Troon, he wins the **The Open.** He is only the third golfer, at that time, to win both Championships in the same year.

1983 A world record was made when two world Heavyweight champions defended their titles the same night, at the same place: Larry Holmes retaining the **WBC** title and Michael Dokes retaining his **WBA** title.

1984 John McEnroe has his best season. He wins 13 singles tournaments, including **Wimbledon** where he loses just one set on his way to his third Wimbledon singles title. This includes a straight set win over Jimmy Connors in the final. He also wins the **US Open**, capturing the year-end number one ranking.

1985 - 1989

1985 In **Super Bowl XIX** the San Francisco 49ers (NFC) beat the Miami Dolphins (AFC) 38–16.

Libby Riddles becomes the first woman to ever win the **Iditarod Trail Sled Dog Race**.

1986 Jack Nicklaus becomes the oldest Masters winner (age 46), and wins his last major golf championship.

At the World Figure Skating Championships the men's champion was Brian Boitano, and Debi Thomas, the Ladies' champion, both from the US.

1987 In **Baseball**, Minnesota Twins pitcher Joe Niekro is suspended for 10 days for possessing a nail file on the pitcher's mound. Niekro claimed he had been filing his nails in the dugout and put the file in his back pocket when the inning started.

1988 **Summer Olympics** takes place in Seoul, South Korea. The US wins 36 gold medals but are 3rd behind the USSR and East Germany.

The **Winter Olympics** takes place in Calgary, where Canada fail to win a gold medal.

The Italian cycle race, the **Giro d'Italia** is won by Andrew Hampsten of the United States.

1989 The world's greatest cycle race, the **Tour de France** was won by Greg LeMond of the US, as well as the **Road Cycling World Championships**.

Associated Press Male Athlete of the Year was Joe Montana of the National Football League and the **Female Athlete of the Year** was tennis star Steffi Graf.

IN THE 1980s

You cannot be serious!

During the 1981 Wimbledon Championships, John McEnroe uttered what has become the most immortal phrase in tennis, if not all sport, when he screamed "you cannot be serious" at a Wimbledon umpire while disputing a line call. Already called "Superbrat" by the British tabloid press for his verbal volleys during previous Wimbledon matches, it was in a first-round match against fellow American Tom Gullikson, who was serving at 15-30 and 1-1 in the first set when a McEnroe shot was called out. Approaching the umpire, he said: "Chalk came up all over the place, you can't be serious man." Then, his anger rising, he bawled the words that would stay with him for a lifetime and find its way into the sporting annals. "You cannot be serious," he screamed. "That ball was on the line".

On the receiving end of the tirade was umpire Edward James, who eventually responded by politely announcing: *"I'm going to award a point against you Mr McEnroe."* It made little difference, McEnroe went on to win in straight sets and two weeks later had his final victory over Bjorn Borg.

The 1998 Canadian Winter Olympics

In 1988, the Canadian city of Calgary hosted the first Winter Olympics to span three weekends, lasting for a total of 16 days. The weather conditions were a problem with temperatures ranging from −18 to 72 °F. After an unexpectedly freezing opening ceremony, the men's downhill skiing was postponed for one day, due to Chinook winds blowing up to 100 miles/hr.

One of the most popular athletes from the games was British ski jumper Michael Edwards, who finished so far behind the others he became an instant celebrity as "Eddie The Eagle", including having a movie starring him. The Jamaican bobsleigh team was also popular having no snow at home to train on!

Canada did not win a gold medal. US won 6 medals, including two gold, with the USSR topping the table with 11 gold and 29 medals in total.

American Car Manufacturing

The 1980s was the golden age for American car manufacturers
The top 10 selling vehicles were:
1. Ford F-Series
2. Chevrolet Cavalier
3. Ford Escort
4. Chevrolet Celebrity
5. Oldsmobile Ciera
6. Ford Tempo
7. Toyota HiLux
8. Chevrolet Caprice
9. Buick Century
10. Oldsmobile Supreme

However lower down the list there is a hint of a rise of imported cars that was to accelerate to this day. The Japanese led the invasion with Toyota, Nissan, Honda, and Mazda. The Europeans were also making a showing with VW, BMW, Audi, Saab, Volvo and Mercedes all in the top 100 selling cars.
Despite being much smaller, these imports had much better fuel economy than most US vehicles and in the decades to come would start to dominate the car market with their economy and quality.

The Ford F-Series was the best seller in 1985

Chevrolet Cavalier was the number 2 seller.

Ford Escort filled the number 3 sales spot.

Chevrolet Celebrity was the fourth best seller.

Buckle Up!

Although Federal Law has obliged vehicle manufacturers to install seat belts since 1965, it was not until December 1984 that the New York state became the first to pass a law requiring all drivers to wear their belts. In spite of a great deal of 'grumbling' and more, ranging from *"the erosion of our civil liberties"*, to *"its uncomfortable, restrictive and creases my clothes"* and horror stories of crash victims being *"hanged"* by their belts or suffering greater injury, 70% of drivers and front seat passengers were observed to be wearing seat belts soon after the law came into effect – and these rates have slowly increased since then. There was an immediate reduction in driver fatalities and a 20 per cent reduction in fatal injuries among front seat passengers.

Many states make it compulsory for everyone over 16 to wear a seat belt in the front seats but only some have it as a requirement in the rear seats. Child seats are widely recommended but whilst some states specify safety seats and/or booster seat others do not. Most researchers conclude that child safety seats offer a considerable safety advantage over seat belts alone

IN THE 1980s

Aviation

Flying started to become more common place in the 1980s with the coach class cabin looking much as it does today. Lavish, multi-course meals had been mostly replaced with more humble dinners served from boxes or trays.

In 1988 for the first time, smoking was prohibited on US domestic flights of less than two hours. Just a year later, the law was extended to flights of six hours, which applied to almost every flight across the country. This smoking ban wasn't adopted internationally until 2000.

Motorcycles

The Japanese brands were now the power in the industry. In the USA, dominant brands like Harley-Davidson were in trouble despite President Regan introducing import tariffs.

Only 3000 Honda FVR750R motorcycles were made, race bred machines with lights thrown on to make them road legal and sold to the public. The first batch of 1000 sold out instantly. With a top speed of 153mph the V-four powered RC30 was one of the fastest sports bike of the decade.

The Dallas Area Rapid Transit (DART)

Created in 1983, DART set out to change commuting, specifically aiming to reduce car usage by building a new network of buses, light rail, and high occupancy only vehicle lanes across 13 cities in the Dallas-Fort Worth area.

The area served is 700 square miles and comprises:
• 629 buses
• 93 miles of light rail with 65 stops which is the largest in the United States
• 34 miles of commuter rail with 10 stations
• A small street car system
• There are up to 250,000 users each day

While a success, DART needs to be subsidised through a sales tax and has not prevented the regions roads from becoming increasingly busy as this part of Texas continues to attract businesses and people from other states due to its good climate and low rates of taxation.

1990 - 1994

1990:

Jan: Douglas Wilder becomes the first elected African American governor as he takes office in Richmond, Virginia.

Feb: Nelson Mandela is released from prison in South Africa, after 27 years behind bars.

Oct: Cold War: East Germany and West Germany reunify into a single Germany.

1991:

Jan: The Gulf War begins, with bombing on Iraq supported by the British Royal Air Force.

Feb: Gulf War: An Iraqi missile hits an American military barracks in Saudi Arabia, killing 29 U.S. soldiers and injuring 99 more.

July: Apartheid ends in South Africa. They are readmitted to the Olympics and the next day, the US terminates sanctions on South Africa.

1992:

Apr: The acquittal of four police officers in the Rodney King beating criminal trial, triggers massive rioting lasting 6 days in Los Angeles, resulting in 63 deaths and over $1 billion in damages.

Nov: Democrat Bill Clinton is elected as the next President of the US.

Dec: U.S. military forces land in Somalia.

1993:

Jan: US$7.4 million is stolen from the Brink's Armored Car Depot in Rochester, New York.

March: The Great Blizzard of 1993 hits eastern U.S., with record snowfall and other severe weather killing 184 people.

Oct: In Mogadishu, Somalia, The U.S. Army has two Blackhawks shot down with over 74 Americans wounded, 18 killed and 1 captured. This prompts the film "Blackhawk Down"

1994:

Jan: The Northridge earthquake strikes Greater Los Angeles leaving 57 people dead and more than 8,700 injured.

Record cold temperatures hit the eastern United States. The coldest temperature ever measured in Indiana state history, −36 °F is recorded in New Whiteland, Indiana.

Amazon was founded in Seattle on July 5, 1994, by Jeff Bezos. Amazon went public in May 1997 and began selling music and videos in 1998. The following year, it began selling music, video games, consumer electronics, home improvement items, software, games, and toys.

1991: The internet already existed but no one had thought of a way of how to link one document directly to another until in 1989, British scientist Tim Berners-Lee, invented the WorldWideWeb. The www. was introduced in 1991 as the first web browser and the first website went online in August.

OF THE 1990s

1996: At the height of the climbing season on Mount Everest a major blizzard swept in. There were several climbing teams high on the mountain and they immediately began to descend to the South Col. Eight guides, clients and sherpas died that day, but the storms continued and eventually the season claimed 24 lives, making it the deadliest season so far.

Before this, most Everest climbers were highly experienced professionals, but 1996 year saw many less experienced amateurs who were paying an expedition group to be taken up the mountain. Was this a contributing reason why so many died?

1999: On 1st January, the new European currency, the Euro is launched and some 320 million people from eleven European countries begin carrying the same money in their wallets.

Britain's Labour government preferred to stay with the pound sterling instead.

1995:

Apr: 168 are killed and 680 wounded in the Oklahoma City by a bomb set off by Timothy McVeigh.

June: U.S. astronaut Norman Thagard breaks NASA's space endurance record of 14 days, 1 hour and 16 minutes, aboard the Russian space station Mir.

Sept: Sony releases the PlayStation to enter the North American video game market.

1996:

Feb: In the UK, the Prince and Princess of Wales agree to divorce more than three years after separating.

Aug: After a 3-year-old boy falls into the 20-foot deep gorilla enclosure at Brookfield Zoo, Chicago, Binti Jua, a female lowland gorilla sits with the injured boy until his rescue.

1997:

Jan: Bill Clinton is sworn in for a second term as President of the United States.

May: The 8 mile long Confederation Bridge, the world's longest bridge spanning ice-covered waters, opens between Prince Edward Island and New Brunswick, Canada.

Aug: Princess Diana is killed in a car crash in Paris. Dodi Fayed, the heir to the Harrods empire is killed with her

1998:

Apr: The Good Friday Agreement between the UK and Irish governments is signed.

Aug: The bombing of the U.S. embassies in Dar es Salaam, Tanzania, and Nairobi, Kenya, by terrorists linked to Osama bin Laden, kill 224 people and injure over 4,500;.

1999:

Feb: President Bill Clinton is acquitted in impeachment proceedings.

July: American soccer player Brandi Chastain scores the winning penalty kick against China in the final of the FIFA Women's World Cup.

THE HOME

Home life in the 1990s was changing again. Family time was not cherished as it had once been, children had a lot more choice and were becoming more independent with their own TVs programmes, personal computers, music systems, mobile phones and the introduction of the world wide web, which meant life would never be the same again.

After school and weekend organised activities for the young spread, with teenagers able to take advantage of the fast-food chains, or eating at different times, meaning no more family eating together. Families 'lived in separate' rooms, there were often two televisions so different channels could be watched and children wanted to play with their Nintendos or listen to their Walkmans in their own rooms which were increasingly themed, from Toy Story to Athena posters, a ceiling full of sticker stars that illuminated a room with their green glow and somewhere in the house, room had to be made for the computer desk.

Track lighting was an easy way to illuminate a room without relying on multiple lamps and it became a popular feature in many '90s homes along with corner baths – most of which also had a water jet function which suddenly turned your bath into a low-budget Jacuzzi!

71% of households owned at least one car, and the use of 'out of town' supermarkets and shopping malls, where just about anything and everything could be purchased in the same area, meant that large weekly or even monthly shops could be done in a single outing. Combined with the huge increase in domestic freezers and ready prepared foods, time spent in the kitchen and cooking could be greatly reduced. Malls became leisure destinations and provided air conditioned relief from winter cold and summer heat.

Over 80% of households owned a washing machine and 50%, a tumble dryer, so the need to visit the laundromat all but disappeared and instead of "Monday is washing day", the family's laundry could be carried out on an 'as and when' basis. All contributing to an increase in leisure time.

Over 80% of homes had microwaves and for working families who did not want to do their own cleaning, many professional companies such as Molly Maids, Merry Maids, the Maids and MaidPro were created to provide a service doing these chores for time poor people.

Commuting

Increased car ownership meant that people could live further and further away from the city. Only in a few cities like New York or San Francisco was public transport popular. Car drivers faced longer and longer journey times to work, but they listened to the radio or the cassette player, were in an air-conditioned space and did not have to worry about who they were sat next to!
The smallest breakdown or accident could cause massive jams and hold ups.

ART AND CULTURE

1990 - 1994

1990 In Rome, on the eve of the final of the FIFA World Cup, the Three Tenors sing together for the first time. The event is broadcast live and watched worldwide by millions of people. The highlight is Luciano Pavarotti's performance of Nessun Dorma.

1991 Guardians of the Gate is a 1991 Everdur bronze sculpture depicting a family of sea lions by Miles Metzger, located northwest of Pier 39 and adjacent to the Embarcadero Center in San Francisco.

1992 Herbert and Dorothy Vogel collection, one of the most important post-1960s art collections in the United States, is given to National Gallery of Art in Washington, D.C.

1993 The comic book collecting boom achieves its peak in 1992 fuelled by "The Death of Superman" which followed on from the success of the movie Batman.
Roy Lichtenstein, the American pop artist, produced "Large Interior with Three Reflections".

1994 Restoration of the Sistine Chapel frescoes: Michelangelo's The Last Judgment in the Sistine Chapel (Vatican City) is reopened to the public after 10 years of restoration. Colors and details that had not been seen for centuries were revealed.

1995 - 1999

1995 The first ever World Book Day was held on 23rd April, picked to celebrate the anniversary of William Shakespeare's death.
The new San Francisco Museum of Modern Art, designed by Mario Botta, opens.

1996 Leading talk show host Oprah Winfrey became an important book influencer when she launched the highly successful Oprah's Book Club.

1997 The hugely successful Harry Potter series by J. K. Rowling was introduced. The series, with seven main novels, would go on to become the best-selling book series in world history and adapted into a film series in 2001.

1998
More than 15,000 people attend a tribute concert held for Diana, Princess of Wales, at her family home, Althorp Park.

1999 The Petronas Twin Towers, Kuala Lumpur, Malaysia, became two of the tallest man-made structures ever built after they officially opened on August 31.

1997: Harry Potter and the Philosopher's Stone' by J.K. Rowling made its debut in June. The initial edition of this first book in the series, comprised 500 copies and the novel has gone on to sell in excess of 120 million. The success of the whole Harry Potter phenomenon is well known, and there have been less expected benefits too. Certainly, before the films, children loved reading the books and boosted the reported numbers of children reading and indeed, reading longer books.

The perception of boarding schools, often associated with misery and cruel, spartan regimes was changed for some by Hogwarts School of Witchcraft and Wizardry. The sense of excitement, community and friendship of the children, the camaraderie of eating together and playing together, made going away to school more appealing for many.

The amazing visual effects used in the films were instrumental in persuading Hollywood to consider UK technical studios and raised the number of visual effects Oscar nominations for British companies significantly.

1997: The Guggenheim Museum of modern and contemporary art, designed by Canadian-American architect Frank Gehry, opened in Bilbao. The building represents an architectural landmark of innovating design, a spectacular structure.

The museum was originally a controversial project. Bilbao's industry, steel and shipbuilding was dying, and the city decided to regenerate to become a modern technological hub of the Basque region, and the controversy was, instead of an office block or factory, the centre piece would be a brand-new art gallery.

It is a spectacular building, more like a sculpture with twisted metal, glass, titanium and limestone, a futuristic setting for fine works of art. The gamble paid off, in the first twenty years, the museum attracted more than 19 million visitors with 70% from outside Spain. Foreign tourists continue to travel through the Basque country bringing a great economic boost to the region and Bilbao itself, has transformed from a grimy post-industrial town to a tourist hotspot.

FILMS

1990 - 1994

1990 It was Oscar time for an epic western this year and **Dances With Wolves**, directed and starring Kevin Costner with seven Academy Awards, won Best Picture and Best Director. It is one of only three Westerns to win the Oscar for Best Picture, the other two being **Cimmaron** in 1931 and **Unforgotten** in **1992**.

1991 *"Well, Clarice - have the lambs stopped screaming?"* wrote Dr Hannibal Lecter to the young FBI trainee, Clarice Starling. The thriller, **The Silence of the Lambs**, about a cannibalistic serial killer, scared audiences half to death and won the Best Picture Award.

1992 The nominations for the Academy Awards held some serious themes. **The Crying Game** was set against the backdrop of the 'troubles' in Northern Ireland. There was a blind retired Army officer in **Scent of a Woman**, rising troubles in colonial French Vietnam in **Indochine** and the invasion of Panama in **The Panama Deception**.

1993 The acclaimed **Schindler's List** won Best Picture with stiff competition from **The Piano** which won Best Original Screenplay and Robin Williams as **Mrs Doubtfire** which became the second highest grossing film of the year.

1994 Disney's animated musical **The Lion King** made the most money this year, but **Forest Gump** took the prize for Best and becomes Paramount Pictures' highest-grossing film of all-time. Pierce Brosnan is officially announced as the fifth actor to play James Bond.

1995 - 1999

1995 The tense, amazingly technically correct, story of the ill-fated **Apollo 13** quest to land on the moon failed to win the top Oscar, beaten by Mel Gibson in **Braveheart**, the American take on the story of William Wallace and the first Scottish war of independence against England.

1996 Independence Day the science fiction film focuses on people who converge in the Nevada desert in the aftermath of a worldwide attack by a powerful extraterrestrial race.

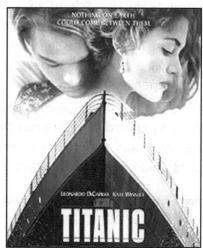

1997 The blockbuster **Titanic** was the film of the year. The combination of romance and disaster proving irresistible. Harland & Wolfe, the builders of RMS Titanic shared blueprints they thought were lost with the crew to produce the scale models, computer-generated imagery and a reconstruction of the ship itself, to re-create the sinking.

1998 Shakespeare in Love, a fictional love affair between Shakespeare and Viola de Lesseps while he is writing Romeo and Juliet was hugely popular and won seven Oscars.

1999 In **American Beauty,** Kevin Spacey plays Lester Burnham, an unhappy executive whose midlife awakening is the crux of the story. Bad as he thinks his life is, he cannot not stop seeing the beauty of the world around him.

**"Fear can hold you prisoner,
Hope can set you free."**

In 1994, Tim Robbins and Morgan Freeman starred in **The Shawshank Redemption**, an inspirational, life-affirming and uplifting, old-fashioned type of prison film and character study in the style of 'The Birdman of Alcatraz'. Set in a fictional, oppressive Shawshank State Prison in Maine, two imprisoned men bond over the years, in a tale of friendship, patience, hope, survival and ultimately finding solace and eventual redemption through acts of common decency.

The film was initially a box office disappointment. Many reasons were put forward for its failure at the time, including a general unpopularity of prison films, its lack of female characters and even the title, which was considered to be confusing. However, it was nominated for seven Academy Awards, failed to win a single Oscar, but this raised awareness and increased the film's popularity such that it is now preserved in the US National Film Registry as "culturally, historically, or aesthetically significant".

Jurassic Park

This 1993 science fiction action film directed by Steven Spielberg, is set on the fictional island of Isla Nublar, where wealthy businessman John Hammond and a team of genetic scientists have created a wildlife park of de-extinct dinosaurs. When industrial sabotage leads to a catastrophic shutdown of the park's power facilities and security precautions, a small group of visitors and Hammond's grandchildren struggle to survive and escape the perilous island.

The film was backed by an extensive $65 million marketing campaign, which included licensing deals with over 100 companies. *Jurassic Park* premiered on June 9, 1993, at the Uptown Theater in Washington, D.C., and was released on June 11 in the United States. It went on to gross over $914 million worldwide in its original theatrical run, becoming the highest-grossing film ever at the time, surpassing Spielberg's own *E.T. The Extra-Terrestrial*, a record held until the release of *Titanic* in 1997

FASHION

SUPERMODELS

The original supermodels of the 1980s, Linda Evangelista, Naomi Campbell, Christy Turlington and Cindy Crawford were joined later by Claudia Schiffer and then Kate Moss to become the "Big Six". Models used to be categorised as 'print' or 'runway' but the "Big Six" showed that they could do it all, catwalk, print campaigns, magazine covers and even music videos and they became pop 'icons' in their own right. The models were also known for their earning capacity, one famous remark from Linda Evangelista, "We don't wake up for less than $10,000 a day!"

But with the popularity of grunge, came a shift away from the fashion for feminine curves and wholesome looking women, and in came the rise of a new breed of fragile, individual-looking and often younger, models, epitomised by Kate Moss. Her waif-like thinness and delicacy complemented the unkempt look that was popular in the early nineties and a new phrase 'heroin chic' described the down-at-heel settings for fashion shoots presented in magazines. By the end of the decade however, attitudes had shifted and concern about the health of the skeletal model was becoming a source of great debate.

GOTH

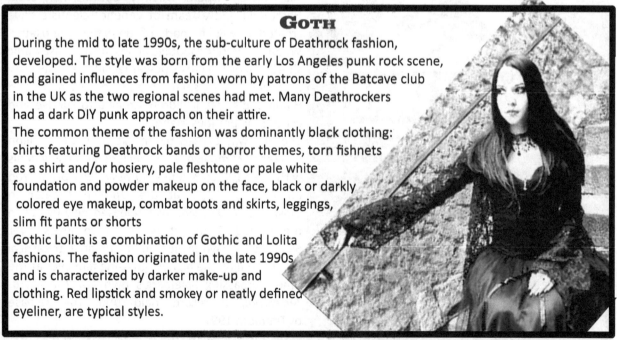

During the mid to late 1990s, the sub-culture of Deathrock fashion, developed. The style was born from the early Los Angeles punk rock scene, and gained influences from fashion worn by patrons of the Batcave club in the UK as the two regional scenes had met. Many Deathrockers had a dark DIY punk approach on their attire.

The common theme of the fashion was dominantly black clothing: shirts featuring Deathrock bands or horror themes, torn fishnets as a shirt and/or hosiery, pale fleshtone or pale white foundation and powder makeup on the face, black or darkly colored eye makeup, combat boots and skirts, leggings, slim fit pants or shorts

Gothic Lolita is a combination of Gothic and Lolita fashions. The fashion originated in the late 1990s and is characterized by darker make-up and clothing. Red lipstick and smokey or neatly defined eyeliner, are typical styles.

In The 1990s

Grunge

Grunge was a style for the young that emerged in Seattle in the late 1980s and by the early 90s had spread across the world. Made popular by bands such as Nirvana, it was a fashion for both men and women. The look was simple, an oversized flannel shirt, sometimes worn over a t-shirt, and baggy, worn out jeans to give an overall, dishevelled, appearance. The clothes were found ideally in charity shops or at the back of "Dad's wardrobe". Black combat-style boots or Converse shoes finished the ensemble.

Nirvana's lead singer Kurt Cobain epitomised the look with holes in his jeans and cardigan sweaters and the fashion world caught on when their second album, 'Nevermind' was released in 1991 and grunge made it onto the catwalk – specifically by Calvin Klein on an 18-year-old Kate Moss. Shrunken baby doll dresses, old prom dresses or even old petticoats and simple slip dresses appeared, often worn with chunky boots and for men, beanies, band t-shirts and knitted sweaters with patterns.

Friends

For women, long loose hair was the most popular women's style, but the most requested hairstyle of the 1990s was said to be 'The Rachel'. Jennifer Anniston's character in 'Friends', Rachel Green, had the haircut people wanted – bouncy, layered, shoulder length, obviously styled to within an inch of its life yet at the same time artfully tousled.

Hoodies

Utilitarian styles such as cargo pants and The Gap's hooded sweatshirts became popular for everyday wear. Industrial and military styles crept into mainstream fashion and camouflage pants were everywhere on the street.
There was also a concerted move towards logoed clothing such as by Tommy Hilfiger

THE GAMES CHILDREN PLAYED

The trend in the 90s was for more electronic, video and computer games but younger children still enjoyed many of the traditional past-times, no single possession could rocket a child to the top of the elementary school social stratosphere quite like a thoughtful, well-balanced sticker collection.

Most '90s kids will remember the pure adrenaline of playing Risk with their friends and family. Risk allowed players to move armies and take over an enemy's territory. For kids, it was the closest thing they came to conquering the world.

The Sega Genesis Console didn't become a popular household item until the early 1990s. One of the most popular Sega Console games was Sonic The Hedgehog which quickly became a cult classic video game that is still played to this day.

However, it was Sony's PlayStation which was the big innovation of the 90s. The first version was able to process games stored on CD-ROMs and introduced 3D graphics to the industry. It had a low retail price and Sony employed aggressive youth marketing. Ridge Racer was the classic motor racing game used in the launch and the popularity of this game was crucial to the early success of the PlayStation.

RESTORATION OF THE SPA

For Native Americans across the continent, hot springs were typically considered neutral ground, where different tribes could come for relaxation, healing, and ceremonies. European settlers soon discovered the springs and their therapeutic properties, and from the late 1700s onward established many spa towns. America's first spa town, tiny Berkeley Springs, West Virginia, was established in 1776.

The 1990s saw the rise of spa resorts combining top-notch spa services and facilities with luxurious hotel rooms, gourmet dining, and a wide range of leisure activities. The emphasis was on pampering rather than healing and this has developed into spas that emphasize healthy living, healthy meals, physical-fitness, weight loss, detoxification and general wellbeing.

IN THE 1990s

WHERE WE WENT ON VACATION

In 1990 the Washington Post said *"Half of all adult Americans expect to vacation outside the continental United States during the next 10 years"*. Booking with a Travel Agent in town or finding a cheap package deal from a brochure, we arrived at our destination with a guide-book, Travellers Cheques and a camera complete with film.

Not only were people traveling across the globe, but the end of communism and the collapse of the Soviet Union allowed many other nations to welcome international travelers. Visiting Moscow, Russia was trendy and the end of the Apartheid meant people could go on safaris in South Africa.

Backpacking was popular amongst the young with a trans Europe trip on a Eurail Pass being the 'thing to do', often before going on to college. They visited London, Paris, Rome, slept in hostels and on beaches and had a great experience.

Others visited India, Pakistan and Nepal, Australia, Thailand, the USA and New Zealand being their favoured countries to visit. Some did voluntary work in the developing nations, building schools and teaching children English.

The 90s saw plenty of new cruise ships being launched for what became a massive growth industry. New cruise lines were formed, and many existing lines merged and Royal Caribbean, Celebrity, Fred Olsen and Carnival, Disney, Silver Sea and Princess lines were all introducing, predominantly older people, to new places and entertaining them royally on the way.

Between 1988–2009 the largest cruise ships have doubled the total passengers (2,744 to 5,400), and tripled in volume with almost every deck having cabins with verandas.

Music

1990 - 1994

1990 Sinéad O'Connor **"Nothing Compares 2U"**, Mariah Carey **"Vision of Love"** and Stevie B **"Because I Love You (The Postman Song)"** each spent 4 weeks at number one.

1991 Cher made the 1960s "**Shoop Shoop Song (It's in His Kiss)**" an international hit once again. "**(Everything I Do) I Do It for You**", from the soundtrack of the film 'Robin Hood: Prince of Thieves' was sung by Bryan Adams and became a huge hit, the best-selling single of the year and stayed at No 1 for 16 weeks.

1992 Boyz II Men **"End of the Road"** spent 13 weeks at number 1, only to be eclipsed by Whitney Houston **"I Will Always Love You"** a soul-ballad arrangement of the song for the 1992 film The Bodyguard.

1993 Mariah Carey**"Dreamlover"** and Janet Jackson**"That's The Way Love Goes"** both had 8 weeks at number 1. "**I'd Do Anything for Love (But I Won't Do That)**" was the song of the year and won Meat Loaf a Grammy Award for the Best Rock Solo Vocal Performance.

I'D DO ANYTHING FOR LOVE
(BUT I WON'T DO THAT)

1994 "**I'll Make Love to You**" by R&B group Boyz II Men spent 14 weeks atop the US Billboard Hot 100. It was also the third best performing song in the 1990s, as well as ranking on Billboard Greatest of All-Time chart. It won the Grammy Award for Best R&B Performance by a Duo or Group with Vocals and was nominated for Record of the Year.

1995 - 1999

1995 Mariah Carey & Boyz II Men **"One Sweet Day"** spent 16 weeks at number 1 and received universal acclaim from music critics, many of whom praised its lyrical content and vocals while calling it a standout track and was ranked first in Rolling Stone's reader's poll for the Best Collaboration of All Time

1996 Los Del Rio **"Macarena (Bayside Boys Mix)** had 14 weeks at number 1 and **"Un-Break My Heart"** by Toni Braxton was declared as the most successful song by a solo artist in the Billboard Hot 100 history in 1998.

1997 Elton John **"Candle in the Wind"** was a tribute single to Diana, Princess of Wales, with the global proceeds from the song going towards Diana's charities. The record is the second highest-selling physical single of all time (behind Bing Crosby's **"White Christmas"** from 1942), and is the highest-selling single since charts began in the 1950s.

1998 Brandy & Monica **"The Boy Is Mine"** spent 13 weeks at the number one spot. Aerosmith **"I Don't Want to Miss a Thing"** was the theme song for the 1998 sci-fi disaster film Armageddon and the best selling hard rock song of the year.

1999 Britney Spears made her debut single with "**...Baby One More Time**" which became a worldwide hit and sold over ten million copies. Santana **"Smooth"** spent the last 13 weeks of the year at number one with Ricky Martin **"Livin' la Vida Loca"**, Jennifer Lopez's debut single "**If You Had My Love**" and Christina Aguilera **"Genie in a Bottle"** all spending 5 weeks at the top.

IN THE 1990s

COOL COUNTRY

Garth Brooks

In the 1990s, country music became a worldwide phenomenon thanks to Garth Brooks, who enjoyed one of the most successful careers in popular music history, breaking records for both sales and concert attendance throughout the decade. The RIAA has certified his recordings at a combined (128× platinum), denoting roughly 113 million U.S. Sales.

A steady stream of new artists began their careers during the mid- and late-1990s. Many of these careers were short-lived, but several went on to long-lived, profitable careers. The most successful of the new artists were Shania Twain, LeAnn Rimes, Lee Ann Womack, Martina McBride, Kenny Chesney, Collin Raye, Faith Hill, and Tim McGraw, while Lonestar and Dixie Chicks were the most successful new groups. Twain's **"Come on Over"** album became the best-selling album released by a female of any genre.

LOVE IS ALL AROUND

Whitney Houston, began singing in church as a child and became a background vocalist while in high school. Her hits included **"All the Man That I Need"** (1990) and **"I Will Always Love You"** (1992) which became the best-selling physical single by a female act of all time, with sales of over 20 million copies worldwide. Her 1992 hit soundtrack **"The Bodyguard"**, spent 20 weeks on top of the Billboard Hot 200, sold over 45 million copies worldwide and remains the best-selling soundtrack album of all time. Whitney Houston is the best-selling female R&B artist of the 20th century.

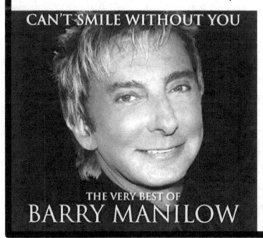

Barry Manilow has recorded and released 51 Top 40 singles including 13 number ones, 28 in the top ten, and 36 in the top twenty. Although not a favorite artist of music critics, Manilow has been praised by his peers including Frank Sinatra, who was quoted in the 1970s as saying, *"He's next."*

In 1998, Manilow released the record album **"Manilow Sings Sinatra"**, a tribute to Frank Sinatra released months after his death, which earned him a Best Traditional Pop Vocal Album Grammy Award nomination in 1999.

SCIENCE AND NATURE

THE HUBBLE TELESCOPE

The Hubble telescope is a general-purpose orbiting observatory. Circling approximately 380 mi (612 km) above Earth, the 12.5-ton telescope has peered farther into the universe than any other before it. The Hubble, which was launched on April 24, 1990, has produced images with unprecedented resolution at visible, near-ultraviolet, and near-infrared wavelengths since its originally faulty optics were corrected in 1993.

Although ground-based telescopes are finally starting to catch up, the Hubble continues to produce a stream of unique observations. During the 1990s and now into the 2000s, it has revolutionized the science of astronomy, becoming one, if not the most, important instruments ever used.

In 1979 the English inventor Michael Aldrich combined a modified TV, a transaction-processing computer, and a telephone line to create the earliest known version of electronic shopping, but it was in the 1990s, following the creation by Tim Berners-Lee of the World Wide Web server and browser and the commercialization of the internet in 1991 giving birth to e-commerce, that online shopping really began to take off.

In 1995, Amazon began selling books online, computer companies started using the internet for *all* their transactions and Auction Web was set up by Pierre Omidyar as a site *"dedicated to bringing together buyers and sellers in an honest and open marketplace."* We now know this as eBay and we can buy just about anything on Amazon.

Comparison sites were set up in 1997 and in 1998, PayPal was founded, the way to pay online without having to share your financial information. By 1999, online only shops were beginning to emerge and paved the way for 'Click for Checkout' to become commonplace.

IN THE 1990s

THE KYOTO PROTOCOL

In December 1997, at the instigation of the United Nations, representatives from 160 countries met in Kyoto, Japan, to discuss climate change and draft the Kyoto Protocol which aimed to restrict the greenhouse gas emissions associated with global warming.

The protocol focused on demands that 37 developed nations work to reduce their greenhouse gas emissions placing the burden on developed nations, viewing them as the primary sources and largely responsible for carbon emissions.

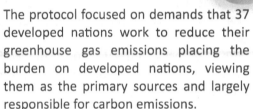

Developing nations were asked only to comply voluntarily, exempted from the protocol's requirements. The protocol's approach included establishing a 'carbon credits system' whereby nations can earn credits by participating in emission reduction projects in other nations. A carbon credit is a tradeable permit or certificate that provides the holder

SHOCK WAVES IN CALIFORNIA

The 1992 Landers earthquake occurred on Sunday, June 28 with an epicenter near the town of Landers, California, in San Bernardino County. The shock had a moment magnitude of 7.3, the largest in the 1990s in mainland USA.

Though it turned out it was not the so-called "Big One" as many people would think, it was still a very strong earthquake. The shaking lasted for two to three minutes. Although this earthquake was much more powerful than the 1994 Northridge, San Fernando Valley one, the damage and loss of life were minimized by its location in the sparsely-populated Mojave Desert.

Damage to the area directly surrounding the epicenter was severe. Roads were buckled. Buildings and chimneys collapsed. There were also large surface fissures. To the west in the Los Angeles Basin damage was much less severe.

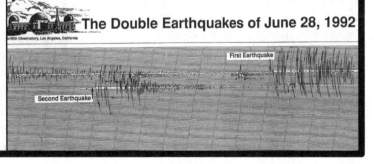

The Double Earthquakes of June 28, 1992

First Earthquake

Second Earthquake

SPORT

1990 - 1994

1990
The British golfer, Nick Faldo, had an amazing year, winning both the **Masters** and the Claret Jug at the **Open** at St Andrews, and capturing the PGA Player of the Year award, the first non-American to do so.

1991 At the **World Athletics** Championships in Tokyo, Mike Powell broke the 23 year-long world record **long jump** set by Bob Beamon, with a jump of 29' 4½".

1992 In the Barcelona **Olympic games**, South Africa competed for the first time since the 1960, Germany sent a single unified team for the first time since 1964, and the United States assembled the best basketball team ever possible terming it "The Dream Team", which won gold.

1993 Super Bowl XXVII was between the (AFC) champions Buffalo Bills and the (NFC) champion Dallas Cowboys. The Cowboys defeated the Bills by the score of 52–17, winning their third Super Bowl, and their first one in 15 years.

1994 Tiger Woods becomes the youngest man ever to win the **U.S. Amateur Golf Championships**, at age 18.
George Foreman becomes **Boxing's** oldest Heavyweight Champion at forty-five.

1995 - 1999

1995 .
Doug Swingley of Montana won the **Iditarod Trail Sled Dog Race** across Alaska. He followed it by winning in 1999, 2000, and 2001. He competed in every Iditarod from 1992 to 2002, and is the only winner from the lower 48 states and second in number of wins.

1996
Chicago Bulls win the **NBA Finals** 4 games to 2 over the Seattle SuperSonics, after a record-breaking 72-10 regular season.
The 122nd **Kentucky Derby** was the 17th year in a row that the favorite failed to win the race. The winning horse was Grindstone.

1997 At 21, Tiger Woods becomes the youngest **Masters** winner in history, as well as the first non-white winner at Augusta. He set the scoring record at 270 and the record for the largest margin of victory at 12 strokes.

1998
World Series Baseball The New York Yankees win 4 games to 0 over the San Diego Padres.

1999
In the **US Open Tennis** final, at the age of 17, Serena Williams beats the number one player Martina Hingis and marks the beginning of one of the most dominant careers in the history of women's tennis.

In The 1990s

The Dangerous Side To Sport

By 1993, Monica Seles, the Serbian-American tennis player, had won eight Grand Slam titles and was ranked No. 1 in the world. On April 30, 1993, then just 19, she was sitting on a courtside seat during a changeover in a match in Hamburg when a German man, said later to be a fan of the tennis star's German rival, Steffi Graf, leaned over a fence and stabbed her between the shoulder blades with a knife. The assailant was quickly apprehended and Seles was taken to the hospital with a wound half and inch deep in her upper back. She recovered from her physical injuries but was left with deep emotional scars and didn't play again professionally for another two years.

Leading up to the 1994 Winter Olympics, figure skater Nancy Kerrigan was attacked during a practice session. This had been 'commissioned' by the ex-husband of fellow skater, Tonya Harding and her bodyguard. Kerrigan was Harding's long-time rival and the one person in the way of her making the Olympic team, and she was desperate to win. Fortunately for Kerrigan, the injury left her with just bruises – no broken bones but she had to withdraw from the U.S. Figure Skating Championship the following night. However, she was still given a spot on the Olympic team and finished with a silver medal. Harding finished in eighth place and later had her U.S. Figure Skating Championship title revoked and was banned from the United States Figure Skating Association for life.

Also in 1994, Andrés Escobar the Colombian footballer, nicknamed 'The Gentleman' - known for his clean style of play and calmness on the pitch - was murdered following a second-round match against the USA in the FIFA World Cup. This was reportedly in retaliation for Escobar having scored an own goal which contributed to the team's elimination from the tournament.

In 1997, Evander Holyfield and Mike Tyson's fight made headlines after Tyson was disqualified for biting off a part of his rival's ear, an infamous incident that would lead to the event being dubbed "The Bite Fight".

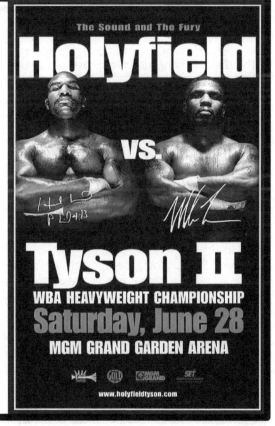

The Sound and The Fury

Holyfield

VS.

Tyson II

WBA HEAVYWEIGHT CHAMPIONSHIP

Saturday, June 28

MGM GRAND GARDEN ARENA

www.holyfieldtyson.com

TRANSPORT

ROAD HAULAGE

The 1990s saw the deregulation of trucking and the industry saw more independent owners and operators. Railways were in decline, especially for short and medium distances where the speed and security of picking up the load from the supplier and delivering it direct to the buyer, was of major importance.

Interstate traffic grew and the relaxing of speed limits in some states also added to the growth of road freight.

CRUISE SHIPS

The largest passenger ship of the 1990s was Royal Caribbean's 'Voyager of the Seas' at 137,276 gross tonnage and 310 m (1,020 ft) long.

This record was held between Oct 1999 and Sep 2000, when it was superseded by 'Explorer of the Seas', larger by only 12 GT. Royal Caribbean have, on order, and due 2024, an Oasis class cruiser of 231,000 gross tonnage, 362 m(1,188 ft) long.

AIR TRAVEL

The days of flying when folks dressed in their Sunday best and were served freshly carved meats from a trolley have long since gone, but air travel in the 1990s was still a very different and often better experience than today. Even coach class meals were served on real crockery with metal cutlery and glassware. Smoking was allowed, drinks were free of charge as was wine with a hot dinner service!

Fares are much lower now and the loss of premium food, service and some comfort has been replaced by planes being the cheapest method of traveling, especially for distances over 500 miles. We also now benefit from a wide selection of in-flight entertainment and the introduction of phones.

Before 9/11, the Transportation Security Administration (TSA) didn't exist. Travelers could go through security with items including liquids, small pocket knives, and wearing bulky jackets. You could also say long goodbyes to family and friends at the departure gate and greet them on their return as they exited the jetway.

IN THE 1990s

Dodge Viper

The Dodge Viper is the true American super car, delivering pure excess in terms of aesthetics, driving experience, and a 440 HP power plant,.

Ford Crown Victoria

The Ford Crown Victoria is the epitome of 1990s American motoring. The #1 preferred car of taxi companies and police departments.

Pontiac TransAm

The TransAm was built and produced by Pontiac from 1967 to 2002. Designed as a pony car to compete with the Ford Mustang delivering 310HP from its 5 lire V8 engine.

Lexus LS 400

Toyota moved into the luxury market with the Lexus brand. The Lexus' flagship model is one of the most reliable vehicles ever built.

COCOTAXI

The auto-rickshaw began in Havana in the 1990s and soon spread to the whole of Cuba. These gas-scooters are named after their shape, that of a coconut and are made of a fibreglass shell with seats welded onto it. They can travel at about 30mph and because they are small, they weave and squeeze in and out of the city traffic. Blue Cocotaxis are for locals, yellow for tourists.

MOTORCYCLES

The Harley-Davidson Fat Boy had been launched in 1990, just ahead of the release of Terminator 2: Judgment Day in 1991. As a result, the Fat Boy became of Harley's best-selling models until this very day. Even Harley's employees attributed the bike's success to the movie, which was itself one of the highest grossing of all time.

NEW YEAR'S EVE 1999
The Millennium Bug

While the world was getting 'ready to party' there was an undercurrent of anxiety about the Y2K (year 2000) Bug and many people were scared. When complicated computer programmes were first written in the 1960s, programmers used a two-digit code for the year, leaving out the "19." As the year 2000 approached, many believed that the systems would not interpret the "00" correctly, making the year 2000 indistinguishable from 1900 causing a major malfunction.

It was particularly worrying to certain organisations. Banks calculate the rate for interest owed daily and instead of the rate for one day, if the 'clocks went back' their computers would calculate a rate of interest for **minus** 100 years!

Airlines felt they were at a very great risk. All scheduled flights are recorded on computers and liable to be affected and, if the computer reverted to 1900, well, there were very few airline flights that year!
Power plants were threatened, depending on routine computer maintenance for safety checks, such as water pressure or radiation levels, the wrong date would wreck the calculations and possibly put nearby residents at risk.

Huge sums were spent to prepare for the consequences and both software and hardware companies raced to fix it by developing "Y2K compliant" programmes. Midnight passed on the 1 January 2000 and the crisis failed to materialise - planes did not fall from the sky, power stations did not melt down and thousands of people who had stocked up on food, water, even arms, or purchased backup generators or withdrawn large sums of money in anticipation of a computer-induced apocalypse, could breathe easily again.

The Millennium Celebrations
The Walt Disney World Millennium Celebration was an event at the Walt Disney World Resort, Epcot with its emphasis on human potential and the possibilities of the future.
In Times Square, New York, a new Times Square Ball made of Waterford Crystal was on display and there was a total attendance exceeding two million spectators. In Madison Square Garden, Billy Joel was performing a special concert and sang a special song titled "2000 Years".

And A New Millennium

Monuments and Memorabilia

National Millennium Time Capsule

"Think of the items, the events and the ideas of the century that you would put into a time capsule, that you think would really represent the United States and the American century: A transistor? [the sounds of] Louis Armstrong's trumpet? A piece of the Berlin Wall? Take any of these items, and it alone could tell a story of the 20th century. It was, after all, the transistor that launched the Information Age, and enabled man to walk on the moon. It was Satchmo's trumpet that heralded the rise of jazz and of American music all over the world. And it was a broken block of concrete covered in graffiti from the Berlin Wall that announced

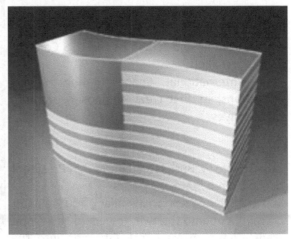

the triumph of democracy over dictatorship. These are just some of the items that will be placed, along with the scores of other objects representing the ideas and innovations that shaped the American century, into our National Millennium Time Capsule."

The Financial Times describes **Chicago's Millennium Park** as "an extraordinary public park that is set to create new iconic images of the city", and it is "a genuinely 21st-century interactive park [that] could trigger a new way of thinking about public outdoor spaces".

The park, opened in 2004 to celebrate the third millennium, features a variety of public art, outdoor spaces and venues. In 2017, Millennium Park was the top tourist destination in Chicago and in the Midwest, and placed among the top ten in the United States, with 25 million annual visitors

The park is praised as a "showcase of art and urban design" by the San Francisco Chronicle.

A lot of memorabilia was produced to mark the new millennium.
Some pieces are timeless classics and others will soon be forgotten.

KEY EVENTS

2000:

March: The Sony PlayStation 2 releases in Japan, and sells over 155 million units around the world before being discontinued in 2013

Oct: Al-Qaeda suicide bombs the USS Cole; 17 sailors are killed

Nov: International Space Station begins operations; its first crew, composed of three men, arrives.

2001:

Jan: George W. Bush is inaugurated as President of the United States.

Sept: Al-Qaeda terrorists hijack four planes, crashing two into the twin towers of the World Trade Center in New York City, one into the Pentagon and one on the outskirts of Stonycreek Township, Pennsylvania.

Oct: The USA invades Afghanistan and topples the Taliban regime, resulting in a long-term war. Steve Jobs introduces the first iPod.

2002:

Jan: The Euro is officially introduced in the Euro zone countries.

Feb: Tom Brady leads the New England Patriots to win their first Super Bowl; during a nearly two decade span, they would appear in ten, winning seven.

March: SpaceX is founded by Elon Musk.

Nov: The 2002-2004 SARS outbreak began in Guangdong, China.

2003:

Feb: Space Shuttle Columbia disintegrates upon reentry, killing all 7 astronauts on board.

Mar: The United States, along with coalition forces primarily from the United Kingdom, initiates war on Iraq

Dec: The Lord of the Rings: The Return of the King is released.

2004:

Feb: Facebook is formed by Mark Zuckerberg and colleagues.

Dec: Sony Computer Entertainment launches the PlayStation Portable.

Dec: Boxing Day Tsunami occurs in the Indian Ocean, leading to the deaths of 230,000.

TERRORISM

2001: On the 11th September, Al-Qaeda terrorists hijack civilian airliners and fly two into the Twin Towers of the World Trade Centre in New York, which collapse. There are 3,000 fatalities including 67 British nationals.

SOCIAL MEDIA

2004: In February, Mark Zuckerberg launches 'The Facebook', later renamed 'Facebook' as an online social networking website for Harvard University Students. In 2006 it was opened up to anyone over the age of 13.

TESLA THE FIRST COMMERCIAL ELECTRIC VEHICLE

2008: Tesla Roadster launched. The company is named after inventor Nikola Tesla. Elon Musk has served as CEO since 2008. Up to 2023 Tesla cars are the biggest selling plug-in electric car worldwide, but is under increasing competition from Ford, GM, VW, and many new Chinese manufacturers.

THE FIRST SMARTPHONE

2007: The iPhone was the first mobile phone with multi-touch technology. The iPhone and the Android competitors, created a large market for smartphone apps, or "app economy". There are many millions of apps now available covering every possible user need from shopping, eating, travel and health monitoring.

2005:
Feb: The Kyoto climate change Protocol comes into effect.**Apr**: Prince Charles marries Camilla Parker Bowles at a private ceremony at Windsor Guildhall.
July: The Provisional Irish Republican Army (IRA) ends its paramilitary campaign in Northern Ireland.
Aug: Hurricane Katrina devastates much of the U.S. Gulf Coast from Louisiana to the Florida Panhandle killing an estimated 1,836 people.

2006:
Mar: Twitter is launched, becoming one of the largest social media platforms in the world.
Mar: Spotify is launched to become one of the largest music streaming service providers.
Dec: Gerald Ford, the 38th president dies aged 93.

2007:
Jan: Nancy Pelosi becomes the first female Speaker of the House of Representatives.
Jan: The iPhone was introduced by Apple with annual new iPhone models and iOS updates.
Apr: During the Virginia Tech shooting, two South Koreans used semi automatic pistols to kill 32 people and wound 17 others.

2008:
Feb: Tesla Roadster launched, the first mass production lithium-ion battery electric car.
Sept: Google Chrome web browser was trested.
Nov: Barack Obama is elected to become the first black President of the United States.

2009:
Jan: The cryptocurrency Bitcoin is launched.
Jan: US Airways Flight 1549 ditches in the Hudson River in an accident that becomes known as the "Miracle on the Hudson", as all 155 people on board are rescued.
Apr: Swine flu pandemic began in North America, rapidly spreading worldwide.

2010:

Jan: A 7.0 magnitude earthquake in Haiti kills 230,000.

Jan: Apple launch the iPad

April: The B.P. oil spill, the largest in US history occurs in the Gulf of Mexico.

June: The FIFA Soccer World Cup is held in Africa for the first time.

2011:

Feb: An earthquake of 6.3 magnitude devastates Christchurch, New Zealand. Hundreds of people are killed.

March: A 9.0 earthquake in Japan triggers a tsunami and the meltdown of the Fukushima Nuclear Power Plant.

April: Wedding of Prince William and Catherine Middleton.

2012:

March: The Encyclopaedia Britannica stops the print edition, 246 years after its first publication.

Jul: The summer Olympic Games are held in London, making it the first city to host them for a third time.

Oct: Skydiver Felix Baumgartner becomes the first person to break the sound barrier without a vehicle.

Nov: Barack Obama wins second term as President of the United States.

2013:

Jul: Uruguay becomes the first country to fully legalize cannabis.

Dec: Death and state funeral of Nelson Mandela in South Africa.

2014:

Mar: England's Prince Harry launches the Invictus Games for wounded soldiers.

June: An Ebola epidemic in West Africa infects nearly 30,000 people and results in the deaths of over 11,000.

Aug: The shooting of African-American teenager Michael Brown by police, leads to violent unrest in Ferguson, Missouri.

THE ROYAL WEDDING

2011: The wedding of Prince William and Catherine Middleton took place on Friday, 29 April at Westminster Abbey in London, England. The groom was second in the line of succession to the British throne. The couple had been in a relationship since 2003. Thousands of street parties were held throughout the UK and millions watched on TV.

THE ARAB SPRING

2010: 'The Arab Spring', a series of anti-government protests, uprisings, and armed rebellions spread across much of the Arab world. Starting in Tunisia it spread to Libya, Egypt, Yemen, Syria and Bahrain. Amongst leaders to be deposed was Gaddafi of Libya.

THE ONE WORLD TRADE CENTRE

2015: One World Trade Center, is the main building of the rebuilt World Trade Center complex in Lower Manhattan, and became the tallest building in the United States, the tallest building in the Western Hemisphere, and the seventh-tallest in the world. The supertall structure has the same name as the North Tower of the original World Trade Center, which was destroyed in the terrorist attacks of September 11, 2001.

GREAT AMERICAN ECLIPSE

The solar eclipse during totality, seen from outside Crowheart, Wyoming.

2017: The solar eclipse of August 21, was a total solar eclipse visible within a band that spanned the contiguous United States from the Pacific to the Atlantic coasts. It was also visible as a partial solar eclipse from as far north as Nunavut in northern Canada to as far south as northern South America.

2015:
June: China announces the end of One-Child policy after 35 years.
Dec: The Climate Conference in Paris agreed to work towards zero CO_2 emissions sometime between 2030 and 2050.

2016:
Jun: Barack Obama becomes the first U.S. president to visit Cuba since Calvin Coolidge in 1928.
Jul: The people of the United Kingdom vote to leave the European Union
Nov: Donald Trump becomes US President.

2017:
July: Russia and China urge North Korea to halt its missile and nuclear programs after it successfully tested its first intercontinental ballistic missile.
Aug: A solar eclipse passes throughout the contiguous United States for the first time since 1918.
Oct: 60 people are killed in a mass shooting at a music festival in Las Vegas.

2018.
May: Prince Harry marries the actress Meghan Markle in St George's Chapel, Windsor Castle, UK. It is thought 1.9 billion people watched on TV worldwide.
June: The first summit between the US and North Korea and the first ever crossing of the Korean Demilitarized Zone by a North Korean leader occur.

2019:
April: A major fire engulfs Notre-Dame Cathedral in Paris, resulting in the roof and main spire collapsing.
July: Mexican Joaquín "El Chapo" Guzmán, found guilty of drug trafficking, money laundering and murder is sentenced to 30 years in prison.
Oct: NASA astronauts Jessica Meir and Christina Koch conduct the first all-female spacewalk outside of the International Space Station.

"One Ring to Rule Them All'

Based on the fantasy, adventure epics written by JRR Tolkein in the 1930s and 40s, Peter Jackson's trilogy of films became a major financial success, received widespread acclaim and is ranked among the greatest film trilogies ever made. The three films were shot simultaneously in Jackson's native New Zealand between 1999 and 2000 and with a budget of $281m, was one of the most ambitious film projects ever undertaken.

The **Lord of the Rings: The Fellowship of the Ring** was nominated for 13 Oscars and won four, one of which, unsurprisingly, was for the Special Effects as did **The Lord of the Rings: The Two Towers** and **The Lord of the Rings: The Return of the King**.

Peter Jackson then went on to make a further three films based on Tolkein's Middle Earth saga, **'The Hobbit: An Unexpected Journey**, **The Hobbit: The Desolation of Smaug** and **The Hobbit: The Battle of the Five Armies**. The three films were prequels to the Lord of the Rings saga and together, the six films became one of the 'greatest movie series franchise' of all time.

'The Greatest Fairy Tale Never Told'

In 2002, the Oscar for Best Animated Feature was awarded for the first time to **Shrek**, the large, surly, sarcastic, wisecracking, Scottish-accented greenish ogre with a round face and stinky breath who took a mud shower outdoors near his home in the swamp and blew fart bubbles in a mud pool! But being a goodhearted ogre, children and adults alike, loved him!

'A Film of Our Times'

The Social Network made in 2010, is an intense biographical drama portraying the founding of the social networking phenomenon Facebook and the resulting lawsuits. Based on the book, 'The Accidental Billionnaires' by Ben Mezrich.

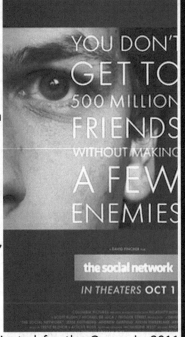

The film was nominated for the Oscars in 2011 winning The Best Adapted Screenplay but missing out on Best Picture to **The King's Speech.**

In The 21st Century

'Precious Pieces'

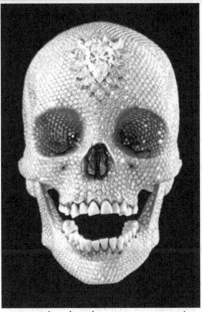

In 2007 Damien Hirst wowed the art-world with his fabulous **For the Love of God** a life-size platinum cast of an eighteenth century human skull, covered by 8,601 flawless diamonds, inset with the original skull's teeth. At the front of the cranium is a 52.4 carat pink diamond. The work is reputed to be the most expensive contemporary artwork ever made and was *allegedly* entitled **For the Love of God** in response to a question posed by the artist's mother "For the love of God, what are you going to do next?"! It has become one of the most widely recognised works of contemporary art and represents the artist's continued interest in mortality and the fragility of life.

Screaming Success

In May, 2012, a pastel version of **The Scream**, by Norwegian painter Edvard Munch, sells for $120m in New York City, setting a new world record for a work of art at auction.

'Question Everything, Believe Nothing'

Conspiracy theory is not a new phenomenon but in 2001, Dan Brown introduced the world to Robert Langdon and a whole new collection of conspiracies and secret societies, with his first book, **Angels & Demons**. Set in the Vatican and Rome, Langdon must decipher a labyrinthine trail of ancient symbols if he is to defeat the Illuminati, a monstrous secret brotherhood.

When **The Da Vinci Code** came along in 2003, hordes of tourists descended on Paris, staring at the Mona Lisa as though she held the secret to life and traipsing around cathedrals and monuments, speculating on the Holy Grail and obsessed with the Priory of Sion and Opus Dei.

By 2009 in **The Lost Symbol**, Brown had set his sights on the Capitol Building, Washington DC and the shadowy, mythical world in which the Masonic secrets abound.

Back in Italy in 2013, this time Florence, for **Inferno**, Langdon is also back to hidden passageways and ancient secrets that lie behind historic facades, deciphering a sequence of codes buried deep within Renaissance artworks with only the help of a few lines from Dante's Inferno.

DAN BROWN

The phenomenal international bestseller

The Da Vinci CODE

CONTAINS PREVIEW OF INFERNO

DAN BROWN

COMING MAY 2013

'Blockbuster perfection'
NEW YORK TIMES

MUSIC & FASHION

First of the Century

The first No 1 Single of the 21st Century in the US Charts is "What a Girl Wants" by **Christina Aguilera**. This song is from her self-titled debut album released in 1999.

The song became her second consecutive US Billboard Hot 100 number-one single, and also topped the charts in Brazil, Canada, New Zealand, and Spain.

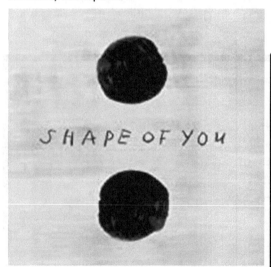

Since 2014 streaming has counted towards sales, called "combined sales", at the rate of 100 streams equal to one download or physical purchase, although the singles chart no longer uses this ratio. The biggest selling song of the 21st Century, based on combined physical, download and streaming sales, *and as of Sep 2017*, is **The Shape of You** by Ed Sheeran, (2017) with sales of just over 3 million.

The Top Ten US Singles 2000-2019

YEAR

2000 **Destiny's Child**: "Independent Women"
2001 **Janet**: "All For You"
2002 **Eminem**: "Lose Yourself"
2003 **Beyoncé** featuring Sean Paul: "Baby Boy"
2004 **Usher** featuring Lil Jon and Ludacris: "Yeah!"
2005 **Mariah Carey**: "We Belong Together"
2006 **Beyoncé**: "Irreplaceable"
2007 **Rihanna** featuring Jay-Z: "Umbrella"
2008 **Flo Rida** featuring T-Pain: "Low"
2009 **The Black Eyed Peas**: "I Gotta Feeling"
2010 **Kesha**: "Tik Tok"
2011 **Rihanna** featuring Calvin Harris: "We Found Love"
2012 **Maroon 5**: "One More Night"
2013 **Robin Thicke** featuring T.I. & Pharrell: "Blurred Lines"
2014 **Pharrell Williams**: "Happy"
2015 **Mark Ronson** featuring Bruno Mars: "Uptown Funk"
2016 **The Chainsmokers** featuring Halsey: "Closer"
2017 **Luis Fonsi** and **Daddy Yankee** featuring Justin Bieber: "Despacito"
2018 **Drake**: "God's Plan"
2019 **Lil Nas X** solo or featuring Billy Ray Cyrus: "Old Town Road"

Millennial Music

What about the music the Millennials, born in the 80s and 90s, like to listen to? It may eventually fit just as well onto a "best songs of all time" playlist alongside the likes of The Beatles and The Supremes. These are some of the 21st-century pop songs that could stand the test of time and they are all female artists too!

Single Ladies (Put a Ring on It) by Beyoncé. **Umbrella** by Rihanna featuring Jay-Z. **Shake it Off** by Taylor Swift. **Toxic** by Britney Spears. **Rolling in the Deep** by Adele and **Firework** by Katy Perry.

However, those of us 'from the good old days' are not surprised to know, that in 2019, a US study found that golden oldies stick in millennials' minds far more than the relatively bland, homogeneous pop of today. A golden age of popular music lasted from the 1960s to the 1990s, academics claimed. Songs from this era proved to be much more memorable than tunes released in the 21st century.

Fashion

Music and fashion have been intertwined since the 1960s and nothing appears to be changing at the beginning of the 21st Century. The young will imitate their idols. Today though, designers are taking their inspiration from the past and bringing it back into the future, the new millennium fashion is a 'fusion' of the 60's, 70's and 80's, feeding our freedom to 'wear what we want, whenever we want'.

However, one major shift of emphasis will be the consumer's demand for environmental sustainability and social responsibility and to move away from 'fast, disposable fashion'. Fashion began moving at breakneck speeds in the 1960's, and the young wanted cheaply made clothing to follow these new trends. Fashion brands had to find ways to keep up with the ever-increasing demand for affordable clothing and this led to the massive growth in manufacturing being outsourced to the developing world, saving us millions of dollars in labor costs.

In the 21st Century we are aware of dreadful labour practices and the enormous amounts of waste. The industry will need to slow down for the customer mindful of how their clothes are made.

where I shop for SUSTAINABLE FASHION

SCIENCE & TECHNOLOGY

Watch everywhere.

Stream unlimited movies and TV shows on your phone, tablet, laptop, and TV without paying more.

The technological innovations of the first two decades of the 21st century have drastically revolutionized peoples' day-to-day lives. Television, radio, paperback novels, cinemas, landline telephones and even letter writing can be, and have been by millions, replaced by connected devices, digital books, Netflix, and communications using apps such as Twitter, Facebook or Snapchat. We have marvels such as personalized hover boards, self-driving cars and, of course, the smartphone. All commonplace now when just a decade and a half ago most were unfathomable.

Consumers watch films, listen to music, record the day, book holidays and carry out their shopping with a few taps on a screen and even people who have never owned a computer are digitally connected 24-hours a day via their smartphones.

E-readers and Kindle

E-readers have been under development since the 1940s, but it was not until 2004 when Sony first brought out an e-reader, and then, when demand for e-books increased, Kindle arrived in 2007, that they became mainstream. An eBook is a text-based publication in digital form stored as electronic files. E-readers are small, convenient, light and have a huge storage capacity that allows for reading while

ONE

THE CASTAWAYS

kindle

travelling, making electronic notes and character summaries and more. Pages do not exist in eBooks and where the reader is 'up to' is altered depending on what font size and layout the reader has chosen, which means 'your place' is displayed as a percentage of the whole text.

Although it was feared e-readers were the death toll for the traditional book, it appears not to be the case as it seems many people really do like to hold a physical book in their hands, feeling the weight. After all, even Kindle uses a **'bookmark'** to hold our place!

3D Printing

The 3D printer has been around since the 1980s. Now, the know-how is getting used for everything from automobile components to bridges to much less painful ballet slippers, synthetic organs, custom dental work, prosthetic limbs, and custom hearing aids.

In The 21st Century

The Future of Transport

Driverless Cars
Self-driving cars are expected to be on the roads more quickly, and in greater numbers, than was anticipated.

Floating Trains
There are already Maglev – magnetic levitation – trains in use. The Shanghai Maglev connects their Airport with a station on the outskirts of the city. At speeds up to 268 mph.

Hyperloop
High speed bullet trains or transport capsules are being developed to provide unprecedented speeds of 600mph.

Solar Panel Roads
Which also generate electricity are being tested in other countries, France, the US and China as well as on bike lanes in the Netherlands.

Touch Screens

Smartphones, tablets, and even Smartwatches all need one underlying technology without which they cannot succeed. The touch screen, as we know it integrated into consumer products, took off in the 2000s and is now everywhere, homes, cars, restaurants, shops, planes, wherever. Unlike other computer devices, touchscreens are unique because they allow the user to interact directly with what's on the screen, unlike a mouse that moves a cursor.

In 2007, the original iPhone was released and revolutionised the phone industry, its touchscreen can change between a dialling pad, a keyboard, a video, a game, or a myriad of other apps. The Apple iPad was released in 2010 and with it, a wave of tablets from competitors. Not only are most of our phones equipped with touchscreens, but portable computers are too.

2000 Tiger Woods wins the **US Open** golf by 15 shots, a record for all majors.

XXVII Summer Olympics - Australia Sydney, USA wins most gold medals (37) and 93 medals in total.

In **Basketball** Los Angeles Lakers win their first NBA title in twelve years, defeating the Indiana Pacers 4 games to 2.

2001
Venus Williams wins the **Ladies Singles Final at Wimbledon**.
At **Super Bowl XXXV** – the Baltimore Ravens (AFC) won 34–7 over the New York Giants (NFC).

2002 "Lewis–Tyson: Is On". Lewis Lennox won the fight by a knockout to retain the **WBC Heavyweight Boxing** Crown.

2003 Mike Wier becomes the first Canadian and the first *left-handed golfer* to win the **Masters**.
Ladies **World Figure Skating** Champion is Michelle Kwan of United States.

2004 The Olympic games returned to its birthplace when Athens was host for the first time since their modern incarnation in 1896.

The USA headed the medal table with 36 gold and 101 medals in total.

2005 Bode Millar was Men's season champion in the **Alpine Skiing World Cup**
MLB World Series – The Chicago White Sox sweep the Houston Astros 4 games to 0 to win the World Series for the first time since 1917.

2006 Justin Gatlin equals Powell's **100m world record** time of 9.77 seconds in Quatar.
In golf, Europe wins the **Ryder Cup** for the third straight time, defeating the USA 18½–9½.
Los Angeles Lakers star Kobe Bryant scores 81 points in a win over the Toronto Raptors, becoming only the second player in **Basketball** league history to score at least 80 points in one game.

2007
Super Bowl XLI – the Indianapolis Colts (AFC) won 29–17 over the Chicago Bears (NFC).
In **Baseball** Seoul Shrubbery defeat the defend champions Singapore Sushi 1,300-1,212 to capture their first ever Periwinkle Feather while in **Major League Baseball** the 103rd edition of the World Series was a best-of-seven playoff between the National League (NL) champion Colorado Rockies and the American League (AL) champion Boston Red Sox; the Red Sox swept the Rockies in four games. It was the Rockies' only appearance in a World Series.

2008 At the Beijing Olympics, Usain Bolt thundered to victory in the **100m Olympic final** at the Bird's Nest in a world record time. He also broke the world record in the 200m.
The USA won 112 medals, including 36 gold.

2009
Super Bowl XLIII was between the AFC champions Pittsburgh Steelers and the NFC Arizona Cardinals. The Steelers defeated the Cardinals by the score of 27–23 at Raymond James Stadium in Tampa, Florida winning their sixth Super Bowl.

2010 At his debut in the US, Amir Khan, the British boxer retains his **WBA Light Welterweight** title for the second time.

Super Bowl XLIV – the New Orleans Saints (NFC) won 31–17 over the Indianapolis Colts (AFC)

The 94th I**ndianapolis 500** was won by Dario Franchitti. The race celebrated the 100th anniversary of the first Indianapolis 500.

2011 Rory McIlroy fired a 69 in the final round of the **US Open**, breaking the record with a 268 and winning by eight strokes. He becomes the youngest US Open winner since Bobby Jones in 1923.

Serbia's Novak Djokovic won three **Grand Slam** events – the Australian Open, Wimbledon and the US Open – and took over the tennis world No 1 ranking from Rafael Nadal.

2012 At the **London Olympics** USA topped the medal table with 47 gold medals and 104 in total

The cyclist Lance Armstrong was banned for life, and stripped of his seven **Tour de France** titles.

In golf's **Ryder Cup**, Europe defeated USA 14½ to 13½ in a miraculous comeback on the final day.

2013 The **Boston Marathon** was disrupted by a terrorist attack in which two consecutive explosions on the sidewalk, near the finish line, killed three spectators and injured 264 other people. The competition was suspended and many runners were unable to participate in the remainder of the competition.

2014 Nineteen horses started the **Kentucky Derby.** California Chrome coasted to the finish line, winning by 1¾ lengths and getting $1.418 million of the $2.178 million purse.

2015 In Golf, Jordan Spieth led from the start in the **Masters**, shooting a record-tying 270, 18 under, to win his first major at the age of 21. Later in the year he also wins the **U.S. Open.**

2016 The Russian team was excluded from the **Olympics and Paralympics** after, possibly, sport's worst ever doping scandal.

19 year old American gymnast Simone Biles left with four **Olympic** gold medals .

2017 Possibly the **Super Bowl's** greatest ever comeback, provided a record 5th ring for Tom Brady. The New England Patriots rallied from 25 points down to send the Super Bowl to overtime for the first time in its history, and went on to win.

2018 In the **NBA Finals** defending champion Golden State Warriors swept the Cleveland Cavaliers 4-0. It was the first time the same two teams met for the championship four years in a row.

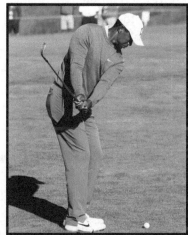

2019

Tiger Woods wins his first major in 11 years at the **Masters**

In the **Kentucky Derby.** Maximum Security led all the way, only to become the first winner disqualified for interference in the race's 145-year history. Country House was declared the winner. Country House paid 65-1,

2020 At the Tokyo Olympics, USA born Lamont Jacobs wins the **100m** sprint for Italy and is the new '**World's Fastest Man**'.

The USA topped the medal table with 39 gold and 113 medals in total.

1974 Tornadoes

Two F5 Tornadoes Strike the Same Place on the Same Day. Since 1900 there have only been 104 of these monsters recorded anywhere on Earth. The United States averages roughly one EF5 per year, but there is great variation from year to year.

The Super Tornado outbreak on April 3, 1974, accounted for seven of the 104 known EF5 occurrences, an anomaly in its own right. Even more amazing, one location in Alabama, near the town of Tanner about 20 miles west of Huntsville, was actually struck twice that day by F5 twisters within 30 minutes of each other.

The first tornado formed at 6:30 pm CDT in Lawrence County and tracked northeast for a full 90 minutes, killing 28 people along the way. Tanner took a direct hit when the twister was at its most powerful, around 7:15 pm. At 7:30 pm the second tornado formed and followed a path almost identical to the first tornado (just 500-1000 yards to the south). Tanner was the first community to be struck by this second tornado, around 7:45 pm. It was on the ground for 50 miles and killed 22. One victim injured near Tanner during the first tornado was transported to a nearby church that was struck by the second tornado, killing him.

"Blizzard Of The Century" March 12-15, 1993

For the first time state governors called states of emergency before even a flake of snow had fallen! The National Weather Service had issued a severe storm warning two days in advance for severe snow from Jacksonville, Florida across 26 states into Canada. Regions where hardly an inch of snow falls in a normal year saw several feet of snow. On the Atlantic seaboard, hurricane-force winds stirred up mammoth swells, and more than 15 homes were swept out to sea on the eastern shore of Long Island.

The storm killed 300 people and caused $6 to $10 billion in damages and these staggering numbers might have been far worse, had it not been for significant advances in U.S. weather forecasting.

WEATHER

Hurricane Katrina 2005

Hurricane Katrina hit the coast of Louisiana on 29th August 2005. A Category 3 storm, it caused destruction from central Florida to Texas, but most lives were lost, and damage caused in New Orleans. It passed over Miami where the 80mph winds uprooted trees and killed two people. Hurricanes need warm ocean water to keep up speed and strength, so Katrina weakened while over the land to a tropical storm. Crossing back into the Gulf of Mexico, it quickly regained hurricane status and at its largest, was so wide, its diameter stretched right across the Gulf.

Katrina crossed back over the coast near Biloxi, Mississippi, where winds were the strongest and damage was extensive. However, later that morning, the first of 50 old levees broke in New Orleans, and a surge of floodwater poured into the low-lying city.

The Dust Bowl Drought of 1934

Scientists from NASA calculated that the 1934 drought extended across 72 percent of western North America 20% greater than the 2012 drought. The Dust Bowl or the Dirty Thirties was a period of severe dust storms causing major ecological, agricultural damage and untold human suffering to American and Canadian prairie areas from 1930 to 1936. Severe drought coupled with extensive farming without crop rotation, fallow fields, cover crops or other techniques to prevent erosion caused the soil to turn to dust, and blew away eastward and southward in large dark clouds.

These immense dust storms "Black Blizzards" reduced visibility to a few feet and millions of acres of farmland became useless, and hundreds of thousands of people were forced to leave their homes; many of these families (often known as "Okies", since so many of them came from Oklahoma) traveled to California and other states, where they found economic conditions little better than those they had left. Owning no land, many traveled from farm to farm picking fruit and other crops at starvation wages. Author John Steinbeck later wrote *The Grapes of Wrath*, which won the Pulitzer Prize, and *Of Mice and Men,* about such people.

GLOBAL DISASTERS OF
Australian Bush Fires

Australia experienced the worst bushfire season ever in 2019-2020 with fires blazing for months in large parts of the country. Around 50,000 square miles of land and thousands of buildings were destroyed and at least 33 people died. Victoria and New South Wales were the worst affected and a state of emergency was declared in the capital city, Canberra.

Australia is used to bushfires, they are a natural part of the country's summer and native trees like eucalyptus need the heat for their seeds to be released, but this season they started earlier than usual, spread much faster, burned hotter and lasted longer, from June 2019 until March 2020, with the worst of the fires happening in December and January.

2019 was Australia's hottest and driest year on record with temperatures hitting 104 degrees and above in every state and these hot, dry and windy conditions made the fires bigger and more intense than normal.

THE INDIAN OCEAN TSUNAMI

In the early morning of December 26, 2004, there was a massive and sudden movement of the Earth's crust under the Indian Ocean. This earthquake was recorded at magnitude 9 on the Richter Scale and as it happened under the ocean, the sea floor was pushed upwards, by as much as 120ft, displacing a huge volume of water and causing the devastating tsunami which hit the shores of Indonesia, Sri Lanka, India, Thailand, and the Maldives.

Within 20 minutes the waves, reaching 30 feet high, and racing at the speed of a jet aircraft, engulfed the shoreline of Banda Aceh on the northern tip of Sumatra, killing more than 100,000 people and pounding the city into rubble. Then, moving on to Thailand, India and Sri Lanka, an estimated total of 250,000 people were killed, including many tourists on the beaches of Thailand. Millions more people were displaced, and eight hours later, and 5,000 miles from its Asian epicentre, the tsunami claimed its final casualties on the coast of South Africa.

THE 21ST CENTURY

Turkish Earthquake

On 6 February 2023, a Mw 7.8 earthquake struck southern Turkey and Syria an area twice the size of Florida. Over 100,000 people died and 1.5million made homeless. In these remote, poor, areas, rescue efforts were slow to get going and like so many poor countries allegations of government incompetence and builders not adhering to earthquake proof standards, were widespread. Over 350,000 apartment blocks collapsed trapping residents.

Some of the trapped sent out cell phone pleas for help, but as help failed to reach them, their cell phone batteries died, along with their vain hopes and their lives.

COVID 19 A GLOBAL PANDEMIC

The first human cases of COVID-19, the coronavirus disease caused by SARS CoV-2, were first reported from Wuhan City, China, in December 2019. Environmental samples taken in a food market in Wuhan where wild and farmed animals were traded, were positive for the virus and it is still unconfirmed whether the market was the origin of the virus or was just the setting for its initial spread.

The virus spread rapidly throughout China and has been found in 202 other countries, reaching USA in 2020. New York had its 1st case on March 1st. By March 22nd 64,258 cases and 491 deaths were confirmed. A week later there were 146,155 cases and 4555 deaths.

Theatres, schools and some businesses closed down. By the end of March 2020 there were over 100,000 cases.

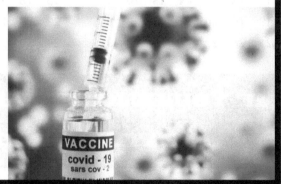

1964 Calendar

January
S	M	T	W	T	F	S
			1	2	3	4
5	6	7	8	9	10	11
12	13	14	15	16	17	18
19	20	21	22	23	24	25
26	27	28	29	30	31	

February
S	M	T	W	T	F	S
						1
2	3	4	5	6	7	8
9	10	11	12	13	14	15
16	17	18	19	20	21	22
23	24	25	26	27	28	29

March
S	M	T	W	T	F	S
1	2	3	4	5	6	7
8	9	10	11	12	13	14
15	16	17	18	19	20	21
22	23	24	25	26	27	28
29	30	31				

April
S	M	T	W	T	F	S
			1	2	3	4
5	6	7	8	9	10	11
12	13	14	15	16	17	18
19	20	21	22	23	24	25
26	27	28	29	30		

May
S	M	T	W	T	F	S
					1	2
3	4	5	6	7	8	9
10	11	12	13	14	15	16
17	18	19	20	21	22	23
24	25	26	27	28	29	30
31						

June
S	M	T	W	T	F	S
	1	2	3	4	5	6
7	8	9	10	11	12	13
14	15	16	17	18	19	20
21	22	23	24	25	26	27
28	29	30				

July
S	M	T	W	T	F	S
			1	2	3	4
5	6	7	8	9	10	11
12	13	14	15	16	17	18
19	20	21	22	23	24	25
26	27	28	29	30	31	

August
S	M	T	W	T	F	S
						1
2	3	4	5	6	7	8
9	10	11	12	13	14	15
16	17	18	19	20	21	22
23	24	25	26	27	28	29
30	31					

September
S	M	T	W	T	F	S
		1	2	3	4	5
6	7	8	9	10	11	12
13	14	15	16	17	18	19
20	21	22	23	24	25	26
27	28	29	30			

October
S	M	T	W	T	F	S
				1	2	3
4	5	6	7	8	9	10
11	12	13	14	15	16	17
18	19	20	21	22	23	24
25	26	27	28	29	30	31

November
S	M	T	W	T	F	S
1	2	3	4	5	6	7
8	9	10	11	12	13	14
15	16	17	18	19	20	21
22	23	24	25	26	27	28
29	30					

December
S	M	T	W	T	F	S
		1	2	3	4	5
6	7	8	9	10	11	12
13	14	15	16	17	18	19
20	21	22	23	24	25	26
27	28	29	30	31		

Made in United States
Troutdale, OR
12/04/2024